Managing
HUMAN RESOURCES
in an Insurance Agency

You're Hired.

You're Fired!

Includes: Sample Employee Handbook, Job Descriptions, Procedures Manual, and a variety of Employment Forms tailored for the insurance industry.

CD ENCLOSED

This publication is designed to provide information in regard to the subject matter covered. It is sold with the understanding that the publisher is not engaged in rendering legal, accounting, or other professional services. If legal advice or other professional assistance is required, the services of a competent professional person should be sought.

DISCLAIMER

You should consult your attorney, accountant and/or other appropriate professionals regarding all human resources practices, subjects, issues, questions, documents, and legal and tax implications.

The book and CD-ROM, and their contents, are <u>not legal or tax advice and should not be considered or applied as legal or tax advice.</u>

The book and the accompanying CD-ROM will provide you with generalized forms, descriptions, citations, procedures and information. These forms and the content of the book and CD-ROM are **MEANT ONLY AS EXAMPLES**; they are not to be used or construed as final products nor copied uncritically. You are advised that you should consult your own lawyer, accountant and other appropriate professionals experienced in all matters contained or discussed in the book and CD-ROM.

There is no substitute for independent thinking and drafting, as each particular situation will pose unique and critical legal, tax and other issues and requirements. Although the author and editors have provided their thoughts and opinions regarding certain such issues and requirements in the context of their practical experiences in view of those experiences and particular circumstances, the thoughts and opinions are not to be construed as legal or tax advice. In each particular situation (for example, each person, particular geographic location, and/or legal, tax, accounting, and business jurisdiction), human resources practices, law and requirements differ; therefore, the book and CD-ROM are intended only for general informational purposes. The information of the book and CD-ROM should not be used, accepted, followed or otherwise considered as authority, instructions, guidance or directions to you, and you should consult your legal counsel and other appropriate professionals as to the information. The author and editors are not responsible for the end product or your use of the information or product.

Foreword

Managing Human Resources in an Insurance Agency fills a special need for the insurance industry. Until now, there have only been human resources books available with general guidelines for business entities in general. This new publication fills a special niche by focusing on the specific procedures and responsibilities of insurance agencies and their staffs. With the attached CD, readers can tailor the enclosed documents for use in their own agencies, with the proper help of an attorney.

Managing Human Resources is the newest addition to the Academy's Productivity Series of publications, helping agencies to operate more efficiently and profitably. The Marketing and Coverage Series are two additional areas of focus for The Academy.

The National Alliance Research Academy serves as the research arm for The National Alliance for Insurance Education & Research. The Academy studies stand on their own as important research and reference works, and also serve to complement National Alliance programs. Alliance programs related to human resources include: Agency Management Practices James K. Ruble Seminar, CIC Agency Management Institute, CISR Agency Operations course, Dynamics of Sales Management, and CRM classes.

The Academy would like to thank the individual Founders and Fellows who lend their support on an annual basis. The Academy also appreciates the contributions of its Research Associates, organizations which support The Academy and assist in the delivery of its publications. Most of all, The Academy extends its gratitude to the author of this book, Jon Persky, CIC, CPA, PHR, who drew from years of learning and experience to produce this publication.

Managing Human Resources in an Insurance Agency should serve as an important tool for insurance agency owners and managers. We encourage readers to give us their comments on this publication and offer suggestions for future research.

Sincerely,

Dr. William T. Hold, Ph.D., CIC, CPCU, CLU
President, The National Alliance Research Academy

Table of Contents

Section 3: Job Descriptions

Section 4: Employee Manual

Section 5: Procedures Manual

Website References

Human Resources Related Courses

About the Author

About the Academy

Academy Publications

Terms and Conditions of Use 200

Section 1: Hiring and Firing

The Cost of Employees

Making optimal use of an agency's human resources is critical since it is the single largest area of expense in an agency. According to the Academy of Producer Insurance Studies' Growth and Performance Standard, between 60 percent and 70 percent of every dollar of revenue taken in by an agency goes out in the form of compensation.

For an agency to maximize its value, it must maximize its profitability, productivity, and efficiency. To do this it must manage its personnel wisely. Yet how much time does a typical agency spend on recruiting, hiring, training, and retaining this valuated resource? Not nearly enough.

Agency owners will complain that they can't find quality employees, yet they continue to use the same methods of recruiting. And while some employee turnover is good, many employers have excessive turnover yet fail to correct the conditions that cause employees to leave.

When it comes to human resources, an agency needs to determine:

1. How many employees does it need?

2. What are these employees going to do?

3. How much is the agency going to pay them?

4. What is the agency going to do in terms of training and development?

An agency's stage of organizational growth will greatly influence the answer to these questions. When an agency is in the existence stage the owner is the agency and the agency is struggling to remain alive. During this phase staff is minimal and the owner does everything he or she needs to in order to obtain and retain clients. Obviously, since there is minimal staffing besides the owner, there is little or no job specialization.

Assuming an agency makes it to the next stage, the survival stage, the agency is an ongoing concern and is trying to generate a profit. Staffing begins to increase. By hiring a CSR, the agency owner can devote more time to sales and marketing which in turn will generate more revenues, which will allow more employees to be hired.

While there has been some staff stratification to free up the owner's time, what about the CSR? At this stage the CSR is handling new and renewal business as well as answering the telephone, handling claims, and ordering supplies.

During the next stage, the success stage, an agency is profitable and even more staff stratification takes place. Perhaps a claims manager is hired to specialize in claims handling. Or an administrative assistant is hired to take some of the clerical responsibilities off the CSR.

Then comes the take-off stage, where an agency is expanding rapidly and targeting new marketing territories. Obviously, additional employees will be needed in this stage. As the agency becomes larger and more profitable it can afford to pay more and offer better benefits. This is also true during the maturity stage when the agency is fully developed and using sophisticated systems.

While paying more and offering better benefits may help to retain employees, it doesn't mean the employees are happy. Many employees have stated "off the record" that they would take another job if they could find a position that pays as well as they are currently making. Is this a good situation? No. The question is, why does the employee want to leave? It may be the work environment or job satisfaction. How is the employee supervised, evaluated, and trained? Failure to do these can result in unhappy employees.

A grave failure many agencies make is to not re-evaluate their organizational structure and employee functions as they move from one stage to the next. Instead, they just add on employees while maintaining the same structure. The typical result is an agency that is not as profitable, productive or efficient as it could be. Personnel planning must be aligned with the overall business plan of the agency.

In addition to the stage of organizational growth, an agency needs to determine what products / services it is going to offer, the level of service it is going to offer, and how it is going to offer this service.

The typical personal lines CSR can handle about $130,000 of commission income. Yet one agency is able to handle $2,000,000 of personal lines commissions with only two personal lines CSRs. How did the agency do this? By being very selective as to which carriers it would utilize. Several decisions were made:

1. Limiting the number of carriers – The agency would only use four carriers. Fewer carriers make the employees more efficient.

2. Upload / Download – To be one of the four carriers, a carrier had to have upload / download capability with the agency's automation system.

3. Direct Bill – The agency would do no billing, so any carrier selected had to have direct bill capability.

4. Service Center – A selected carrier had to have a fully functioning service center because the agency really didn't want to bear the cost of servicing its clients.

Take a look at the math. A typical agency would need 15 personal lines CSRs. Assuming a cost per employee of $35,000 (including taxes and benefits), personnel cost on $2,000,000 was $525,000, leaving a spread of $1,475,000.

But this agency only had two personal lines CSRs that cost $70,000. However, the carriers paid 13 percent commission instead of 15 percent, which reduced commissions to $1,960,000. And since the carrier and not the agency was doing the servicing, retention went down 5%, which brought commission income down to $1,862,000. After subtracting out compensation, this agency had a spread of $1,792,000, over $300,000 greater than the typical agency.

As you can see, service centers will reduce the amount of servicing work done in an agency and also reduce the income of the agency, but this can result in less personnel. Will all agencies be able to achieve the profit of the agency above? No, but judicious use of service centers can increase profit and can have a profound effect on the number of people an agency employs and what functions those employees will perform.

Candidate Sources

The two main sources an agency uses in developing a candidate pool are employment agencies and advertising. Like insurance agencies, there are good and bad employment agencies out there. Which one do you select?

The first issue is whether or not the employment agency specializes in hiring people in the insurance industry. Does the agency understand the different licensing requirements in your state? Do they know the differences in automation systems? Do they understand the typical tasks and functions that occur in an agency? If they do, this should give them a leg up over the typical recruiter. Nevertheless, you should check out the employment agency's references just like you would for an employee.

The next question is, how much will the recruiter charge? It is not unusual for a recruiter to charge up to thirty percent of compensation up to a certain amount. A $30,000 per year employee could cost you $9,000 in fees. In most cases, a recruiter is willing to negotiate fees but you should do this before the recruiter's services are engaged.

Another critical issue is what happens if the candidate doesn't work out? Are you entitled to get some or all of your money back, or is the recruiter merely required to try to find a replacement? Again, negotiate this beforehand, not after the fact.

A list of recruiters that specialize in the insurance industry is available at the National Insurance Recruiters Association webpage www.nirassn.com.

While many agencies still rely on Sunday newspaper ads, thought should also be given to using websites like www.monster.com or www.hotjobs.com. While more expensive than running a newspaper ad, a job website will allow you to attract more candidates from a wider geographic region. But what makes a good classified ad?

Although there are different ad concepts, most classified ads are written with this basic structure:

- Header – Used to attract the attention of the reader. This should entice the reader into reading the rest of the ad. Make it short and to the point. Experiment with different headlines until you find one that works well.

- Body - Interest the reader in your agency and position and cause them to desire to apply for the job. This is where the meat of the ad goes. The objective is to generate a response from a qualified applicant. Be direct and to the point.

- Close – How do they get in touch with you? Do you want them to know who you are? If so, include your agency name, address and / or telephone number. If you include contact information, expect telephone calls. Some agencies decide to place "blind" ads to an unnamed post office box. The problem with that is that some qualified candidates may be reticent to respond.

GROWING INSURANCE AGENCY

Customer Service Rep wanted for fast growing insurance agency. Only those with Property and Casualty insurance experience need apply. Full-time position with excellent benefits and other incentives. Send resume to: **<INSERT CONTACT INFORMATION>**

TAKE OVER EXISTING BOOK

Agency in **<INSERT LOCATION>** is looking for a quality, professional, licensed P&C agent to take over an existing book and build on it. Commercial experience necessary. Excellent benefits and compensation, with bonus potential. Interested parties should email resume and cover letter to: **<INSERT CONTACT INFORMATION>**

A source many agencies overlook is competitors' websites. Make a list of who your larger competitors are. Call their receptionist and ask for their webpage address. Then go look at the webpage. Some agencies try to impress the general public on their webpage by listing the names of all their employees, their credentials, and may even have a picture of them. You now have an instant candidate pool!

A word of warning, if your own webpage lists employees by name it is time to update your webpage and remove that level of detail.

Another great source of candidates is referrals from your existing employees. Your employees may know someone through a former job or association membership. An existing employee is not going to refer someone who will do a poor job; it would reflect badly on that person.

So why not motivate your employees to refer candidates by rewarding them? Recruitment bonuses will motivate the employee and are a lot less expensive than hiring a recruiter. If you are going to have recruitment bonuses, you need to develop a specific program that addresses:

1. How much is the recruitment bonus?

2. When will it be paid?

3. Who is eligible to receive the bonus?

Once these issues are addressed, incorporate them into the employee handbook and develop a recruitment bonus form like the one below.

Exhibit: Employee Referral Bonus Form

Employee Referral Bonus Form

Name of Candidate _____   Phone Number _____

Recommended Position _____

❑ Resume Attached   ❑ Application Attached

I acknowledge that:
1. I must be the first person to refer this candidate to the agency.
2. I am not eligible if I am the immediate supervisor of this candidate.
3. I have read the agency's policy on referral bonuses.
4. Both the candidate and I must be continuously employed by the agency for six months after the candidate's hiring before the bonus will be paid.

Referrer's Signature_____

To be completed by accounting: Amount of Bonus _____ Date Bonus was paid _____

Also, don't forget about utilizing industry associations as a recruiting option. People with industry experience who relocate frequently contact the local Big I or state PIA association for employment opportunities.

Many local National Association of Insurance Women affiliates have an employment chairperson. You can find the local association through the national website: www.naiw.net

Just as in tracking marketing expenses, the agency should keep a record of the methods it uses to find candidates, the cost, and the success rate. Following is a sample form.

Exhibit: Recruiting Method Tracking Form

Source	Cost	Position to Fill	Number of Responses
Newspaper Ad			
Recruiter			
Website			
Current employee referral			
Industry Association			
Other:			

Here Come the Candidates

Once the resumes start flowing in, you should split them into three piles:

1. Interviews

2. Maybes

3. No Ways

The interview pile is contacted to schedule interviews. The "maybes" are for you to take a second look at if no one in the interview pile is a viable candidate. The "no ways" should get a letter or postcard thanking them for their interest but stating they are not candidates. This could also go out to unsolicited resumes as well.

Exhibit: No Interview Postcard

Thank you for your interest in employment opportunities with **<Enter Agency Name>.**

Your qualifications have been carefully reviewed but at the present time no position is available that would utilize your skills and experience.

Your resume will be retained for a reasonable period of time and you will be contacted in the event our employment needs should change.

We appreciate your interest in our agency and wish you success in your search.

Employment Application

Now that you have a source of candidates, you need to start collecting information on them. Having them provide just a resume is insufficient. Make them completely fill out an employment application.

The employment application should include:

Personal Information – Name, address, phone number, social security number as well as questions regarding:

- Eligible to work in the United States

- If they are under 18 years of age

- Criminal convictions

- Reliable transportation

- If they have signed a non-piracy or non-compete agreement

Make sure you do not ask for age or date of birth on the employment application, otherwise a candidate could argue age discrimination. You should gather that information only after you have hired the candidate.

Employment Information – Include name, address, phone number, supervisor's name, employment dates, why they left, and what they did. Any time gaps should be addressed during the interview itself.

Education – Name and address of school, grade completed and subject(s) studied.

Licenses – What insurance licenses do they have?

Designations – Do they have any insurance-related designations?

Software – Address the level of knowledge they have with agency and office-related agency.

References – Gather the contact information for references. Recognize that no one gives the name of someone who will give a "bad" reference and you may need to dig deeper by asking those references who else knows the candidate and then contacting those individuals.

Notification and Agreement – Here is where the agency states that it affords equal opportunity and that agency information is confidential. In the event someone is terminated and doesn't have an employment agreement, a statement about confidential information here can be useful in prosecuting someone who is breaching confidentiality.

Applicant Signature - This is where the candidate states that all the information is true, accurate, and complete. In the event the information is not true, accurate or complete, the agency is reserving the right to not hire the candidate or terminate the employee at any time after he or she has been hired.

All employment applications should be completed prior to the initial interview so that the interviewer can reference the information. The interviewer will need to gather more information than what is on the application. He should screen for indicators of achievement, stability and career direction, time in each position, experience relevant to the position being applied for, and the specific duties the candidate is performing in his or her present job.

If there are frequent job changes or gaps in the candidate's background, they should be fully investigated and evaluated.

The following is a sample employment application that has been tailored for insurance agencies.

Exhibit: Employment Application

Employment Application

Position Applied for _____ Application Date _____

Personal Information

Name: _____
        Last   First   MI

Address: _____
        Street   City   State   Zip

Home phone #: _____ Alternate #:_____

Social Security Number: _____

Are you available to work: ❑ Full time ❑ Part-time _____

If you are under 18 years of age, can you provide required proof of work eligibility? ❑ Yes ❑ No

Have you ever worked or submitted an application with this agency before?
❑ Yes ❑ No If yes, when _____

Are you currently employed? ❑ Yes ❑ No

May we contact your current employer? ❑ Yes ❑ No

Are you eligible to work in the United States? (Proof of eligibility will be required upon employment)
❑ Yes ❑ No

Have you ever been convicted of a crime, excluding misdemeanors? (If yes, attach explanation.)
❑ Yes ❑ No

Do you have a reliable means of transportation ❑ Yes ❑ No

Have you ever been discharged from any employment or been asked to resign?
(If yes, attach explanation.) ❑ Yes ❑ No

Are you bound by any agreement(s) (including signing a non-competition, non-disclosure, or non-piracy agreement)
that would limit your ability to work for the agency?
(If yes, attach copy to this application.) ❑ Yes ❑ No

Page 1 of 5

Employment (Start with most recent employment and work backwards)

Employer	Telephone Number
Full Address (Street, City, State & Zip)	
Supervisor's Name & Title	
Employment Start Date	Employment End Date
Ending Compensation	Reason for Leaving

Describe work performed

_____

_____

Employer	Telephone Number
Full Address (Street, City, State & Zip)	
Supervisor's Name & Title	
Employment Start Date	Employment End Date
Ending Compensation	Reason for Leaving

Describe work performed

_____

_____

Employer	Telephone Number
Full Address (Street, City, State & Zip)	
Supervisor's Name & Title	
Employment Start Date	Employment End Date
Ending Compensation	Reason for Leaving

Describe work performed

_____

_____

Employer	Telephone Number
Full Address (Street, City, State & Zip)	
Supervisor's Name & Title	
Employment Start Date	Employment End Date
Ending Compensation	Reason for Leaving

Describe work performed

_____

_____

Page 2 of 5

Education

Name of School	Address of School	Grade Completed or Degree(s)	Subjects Studied

Licenses

P&C License	❏ Yes ❏ No	State & License #
L&H License	❏ Yes ❏ No	State & License #
Brokers License	❏ Yes ❏ No	State & License #
Series 6 or 7 License	❏ Yes ❏ No	State & License #
Other Licenses	Describe:	State & License #

Designations (Check all that apply)

❏ CIC   ❏ CPCU
❏ CLU   ❏ ChFC
❏ CRM   ❏ CISR
❏ Other_____

Software (Check all that apply)

Software	Skill Level	Version
Microsoft Word	❏ Low ❏ Medium ❏ High	_____
Microsoft Excel	❏ Low ❏ Medium ❏ High	_____
Microsoft PowerPoint	❏ Low ❏ Medium ❏ High	_____
Microsoft Outlook	❏ Low ❏ Medium ❏ High	_____
APPLIED	❏ Low ❏ Medium ❏ High	_____
AMS	❏ Low ❏ Medium ❏ High	_____
Other: _____	❏ Low ❏ Medium ❏ High	_____
Other: _____	❏ Low ❏ Medium ❏ High	_____
Other: _____	❏ Low ❏ Medium ❏ High	_____
Other: _____	❏ Low ❏ Medium ❏ High	_____
Other: _____	❏ Low ❏ Medium ❏ High	_____
Other: _____	❏ Low ❏ Medium ❏ High	_____

References (Please include at least two business and one personal references)

Name	
Company Name	
Full Address	
Phone #	
Occupation	
Relationship	

Name	
Company Name	
Full Address	
Phone #	
Occupation	
Relationship	

Name	
Company Name	
Full Address	
Phone #	
Occupation	
Relationship	

Name	
Company Name	
Full Address	
Phone #	
Occupation	
Relationship	

Additional Experience or Qualifications

List any other experience, skills or qualifications that you believe should be considered in evaluating your qualifications for employment.

_____

_____

_____

Notification and Agreement (Please read before signing)

It is **\<Enter Agency Name\>** policy to afford equal opportunity to all employees and applicants for employment without regard to age, race, religion, color, sex, national origin, marital status or sexual orientation, individuals with a disability, or any other characteristic protected by applicable Federal, State or Local law.

I authorize the investigation of all statements and information contained in this application. I release from liability anyone supplying such information and I also release **\<Enter Agency Name\>** from all liability that might result from making an investigation

If employed, I agree to not engage in any outside activity that would involve a material conflict of interest with, or could reflect adversely on **\<Enter Agency Name\>**. I understand that **\<Enter Agency Name\>** retains the right to solely decide when such conflict exists.

If employed, I agree to hold in strictest confidence any information concerning **\<Enter Agency Name\>**, its Insureds, and its Carriers that may come to my knowledge.

In consideration of my employment, if I am employed, I agree to conform to the employment policies of **\<Enter Agency Name\>**, and understand that my employment and compensation can be terminated, with or without notice, at any time, at the option of either **\<Enter Agency Name\>** or myself. I understand that no representative of **\<Enter Agency Name\>**, other than the President, has the authority to enter into any agreement for employment for any specified period of time, or to make any agreement contrary to the foregoing.

I understand that completion of this employment application does not guarantee that I have been employed by **\<Enter Agency Name\>**.

I certify that all answers given by me are true, accurate and complete, I understand that the falsification, misrepresentation or omission of fact on this application (or any other accompanying or required documents) will be cause for denial of employment or immediate termination of employment, regardless of when or how discovered.

Signed _____ **Date** _____

Page 5 of 5

The Legal Interview

Once you have decided which candidates are potential employees, it's time to bring them in for interviews. Make sure that your selection process provides an equal opportunity for all qualified candidates and that you are not unfairly discriminating.

Make sure that whoever meets with the candidate knows what topics they can discuss and what areas are taboo. For more information on the Federal laws applicable to employment see Section 2 of this book.

Some of the "do's" and "don'ts" of the interview process include:

- Do ask questions that address the candidate's skill and past performance in duties that are related to the ones he / she will perform for you.
  - "Tell me about the most difficult client you ever had to deal with."

- Do monitor interviews to make sure that they only relate to job performance.

- Do the same interview for all the candidates (i.e. ask them all the same questions.)

- Don't ask questions of women or minorities that you wouldn't ask men or a majority group.
  - "Have you ever had an abortion?"

- Don't ask questions which solicit information about religion or national origin.
  - "Where do you go to church?"
  - "Where were your grandparents born?"

- Don't ask broad-based questions that are not related to the job.
  - "What do you like to do in your free time?"

- Don't set unnecessary conditions of employment.

In the event you are unsure whether or not you can ask a question, don't ask it!!!

When the candidate comes in for the interview, make sure that it is in a quiet location and that there are no disturbances unless it is truly an emergency. Since you are going to ask the same questions to all candidates (see above), interviews should all last about the same length of time, at least for the initial round of interviews.

Remember, past performance predicts future performance so the more information you get about the past, the better equipped you are to make an informed decision.

You also need to observe body language. If the candidate isn't making eye contact with you chances are he won't make eye contact with clients. Is that the image you want to project to your clientele?

Two of the more common interview mistakes are the halo effect and the expectation gap. Avoid both at all cost. The halo effect is a tendency to attribute positive characteristics to people we like. If you are an avid scuba diver and so is a candidate, it's nice that you have something in common but not a good reason to hire that person as your receptionist.

Sometimes you are so desperate to hire someone that you tell them whatever they need to hear to get them to accept the position. If what you tell them is not the truth about your agency, there is an expectation gap. The result is a disgruntled employee who will very quickly begin looking for another position.

Checking Out the Candidate

What happens if a newly hired employee drives drunk and kills a pedestrian? Or if a new employee steals money from a client? Can the agency be held responsible? The answer is "yes." It is the concept of negligent hiring.

Take the drunk driver for example. Assume it was a workday, he just had a three-martini lunch, got in a car and killed someone. The victim's family sues the agency. Do you win or lose? It depends.

Did the agency run a Motor Vehicle Report (MVR)? If the answer is "no" and a review of the MVR would have shown a previous DUI, the agency is in big trouble. Had the agency run the MVR and therefore not hired the employee, the employee wouldn't have been in a position to run over the victim.

Negligent hiring is when you hire (or retain) employees who engage in wrongful acts both during and after working hours. As an employer, you have a duty to protect other employees, customers, and visitors from injuries caused by the employee who you should have known posed a risk. Obviously, there are pros and cons to doing more than a cursory background check.

Risks	**Rewards**
• Cost - Criminal background checks can be expensive. • Time spent - Some states can take up to six weeks to confirm a conviction. During this delay you may lose the applicant. • Access - Limited access to records. • Limits – There are legal limits on use of records uncovered. See the Human Resource Law section of this book for more information. • Mistakes - Such as mistaken identity can result in unfair rejection of a qualified candidate.	• Quality – Better applicant pool. • Loss - Reduce theft and embezzlement. • Legal Exposure - Reduce legal exposure for negligent hiring and retention. • Discipline - Potential decrease in discipline problems. • Abuse - Potential to uncover drug/alcohol problems of applicant. • Reduce workplace violence.

Should you do the background check yourself or should you hire an outside party to perform the check for you? There are many qualified third parties that can perform background checks on candidates for you for a fee.

But what should you look for in a background search service? For starters, do not enter into any long-term contracts or contracts with minimums. That way, if you don't like the service you are not tied into that company. Ask for a sample report so that you can determine how easy it is to read a report. And it goes without saying that the company should carry adequate Errors & Omissions insurance.

Some of the things a background search service should look into include:

- Criminal background search

- Verification of prior employment

- Professional license verification

- Credit verification

- Education verification

- Motor vehicle records

- Drug screening

One company that does background searches and also specializes in the insurance industry is The Omnia Group. Information about their background search service can be found at www.omnia720.com/products/backgroundchecks.asp

But let's assume you want to do the background search yourself. What should you do? At the very least, anyone who is going to be driving a car for the agency (regardless of whether it is a company car or their own personal vehicle) should have an MVR run prior to hiring. This should be a condition of employment. Consider using the following motor vehicle record release form.

Exhibit: MVR Release Form

Motor Vehicle Record Release

I understand that driving an <Enter Agency Name> vehicle (or my own vehicle as required) is a requirement of the position I am being considered for and that having and maintaining a satisfactory driving record is a condition of my employment.

I agree to allow <Enter Agency Name> to check my driving record prior to hire and to check it periodically thereafter. I further agree to report any license suspensions, serious accidents or offenses, or any other condition to <Enter Agency Name>'s President within 24 hours after they occur.

I understand that <Enter Agency Name> will use this information for employment purposes only and not furnish this information to a third party without my written consent.

I hereby release <Enter Agency Name>, its employees and those who supplied you with the information from any liability for any damage which may result from furnishing the requested information or my failure to be hired for the position for which I am applying.

_____
Print Name

_____   _____
Driver's License Number   State of License

_____   _____
Signature   Date

In addition to running an MVR, you should also run a credit report on potential hires. Someone with bad credit could be more likely to steal from you, your carriers, or your clients. More information regarding the Fair Credit Reporting Act can be found in Section 2: Employment Law.

Before you run a credit report on a candidate, you need to get his or her permission to run the report. The following is a sample release form.

Exhibit: Credit Information Release Form

Authorization for release of information for employment purposes

In consideration of potential employment with **<Enter Agency Name>**, I, _____ authorize **<Enter Agency Name>** and its designated agents and representatives to conduct a comprehensive review of my background through a consumer report and/or an investigative consumer report to be generated for employment, promotion, reassignment or retention as an employee. I understand that the scope of the consumer report/investigative consumer report may include, but is not limited to, the following areas: verification of Social Security number, current and previous residences, employment history including all personnel files, education, character references, credit history and reports, criminal history records from any criminal justice agency in any or all federal, state or county jurisdictions, birth records, motor vehicle records to include traffic citations and registration and any other public records.

I_____, authorize the complete release of these records or data pertaining to me which an individual, company, firm, corporation, or public agency may have. I understand that I must provide my date of birth to adequately complete said screening, and acknowledge that my date of birth will not affect any hiring decisions. I hereby authorize and request any present or former employer, school, police department, financial institution or other persons having personal knowledge of me, to furnish bearer with any and all information in their possession regarding me in connection with an application for employment. This authorization and consent shall be valid in original, fax, or copy form.

I hereby release **<Enter Agency Name>**, and its agents, officials, representatives, or assigned agencies, including officers, employees, or related personnel both individually and collectively, from any and all liability for damages of whatever kind, which may at any time, result to me, my heirs, family or associates because of compliance with this authorization and request to release. You may contact me as indicated below, I understand that a copy of this authorization may be given to me at any time, provided I request it in writing. Information on this application and results of the background investigation will be maintained in confidence in accordance with **<Enter Agency Name>** hiring practices.

_____

Applicant's Signature   Date

The following information is required by law enforcement agencies and other entities for identification purposes when checking records. It is confidential and will not be used for any other purpose.

Please Print Clearly: Full Name:_____

Address _____
       Street   City   State   Zip

Sex: ☐ Male ☐ Female Birth date _____ Current Driver's License #: _____ State:_____

Other names used:_____ Dates used:_____

In compliance with the Fair Credit Reporting Act, you are entitled to be informed if an adverse action, such as denial of employment, is taken against you because of information obtained from a credit, criminal, or other consumer report it received, and a copy of the FTC notice "A Summary of Your Rights under the Fair Credit Reporting Act." The summary is attached.

Exhibit: Fair Credit Reporting Act Rights Form

A Summary of Your Rights Under the Fair Credit Reporting Act

The federal Fair Credit Reporting Act (FCRA) is designed to promote accuracy, fairness, and privacy of information in the files of every "consumer reporting agency" (CRA). Most CRAs are credit bureaus that gather and sell information about you -- such as if you pay your bills on time or have filed bankruptcy – to creditors, employers, landlords, and other businesses. You can find the complete text of the FCRA, 15 U.S.C. §§1681-1681u. The FCRA gives you specific rights, as outlined below. You may have additional rights under state law. You may contact a state or local consumer protection agency or a state attorney general to learn those rights.

You must be told if information in your file has been used against you. Anyone who uses information from a CRA to take action against you – such as denying an application for credit, insurance, or employment – must tell you, and give you the name, address, and phone number of the CRA that provided the consumer report.

You can find out what is in your file. At your request, a CRA must give you the information in your file, and a list of everyone who has requested it recently. There is no charge for the report if a person has taken action against you because of information supplied by the CRA, if you request the report within 60 days of receiving notice of the action. You also are entitled to one free report every twelve months upon request.

You can dispute inaccurate information with the CRA. If you tell a CRA that your file contains inaccurate information, the CRA must investigate the items (usually within 30 days) by presenting to its information source all relevant evidence you submit, unless your dispute is frivolous. The source must review your evidence and report its findings to the CRA. (The source also must advise national CRAs -- to which it has provided the data -- of any error.) The CRA must give you a written report of the investigation, and a copy of your report if the investigation results in any change. If the CRA's investigation does not resolve the dispute, you may add a brief statement to your file. The CRA must normally include a summary of your statement in future reports. If an item is deleted or a dispute statement is filed, you may ask that anyone who has recently received your report be notified of the change.

Inaccurate information must be corrected or deleted. A CRA must remove or correct inaccurate or unverified information from its files, usually within 30 days after you dispute it. However, the CRA is not required to remove accurate data from your file unless it is outdated (as described below) or cannot be verified. If your dispute results in any change to your report, the CRA cannot reinsert into your file a disputed item unless the information source verifies its accuracy and completeness. In addition, the CRA must give you a written notice telling you it has reinserted the item. The notice must include the name, address and phone number of the information source.

You can dispute inaccurate items with the source of the information. If you tell anyone – such as a creditor who reports to a CRA – that you dispute an item, they may not then report the information to a CRA without including a notice of your dispute. In addition, once you've notified the source of the error in writing, it may not continue to report the information if it is, in fact, an error.

Page 1 of 2

Outdated information may not be reported. In most cases, a CRA may not report negative information that is more than seven years old; ten years for bankruptcies.

Access to your file is limited. A CRA may provide information about you only to people with a need recognized by the FCRA -- usually to consider an application with a creditor, insurer, employer, landlord, or other business.

Your consent is required for reports that are provided to employers, or reports that contain medical information. A CRA may not give out information about you to your employer, or prospective employer, without your written consent. A CRA may not report medical information about you to creditors, insurers, or employers without your permission.

You may choose to exclude your name from CRA lists for unsolicited credit and insurance offers. Creditors and insurers may use file information as the basis for sending you unsolicited offers of credit or insurance. Such offers must include a toll-free phone number for you to call if you want your name and address removed from future lists. If you call, you must be kept off the lists for two years. If you request, complete, and return the CRA form provided for this purpose, you must be taken off the lists indefinitely.

You may seek damages from violators. If a CRA, a user or (in some cases) a provider of CRA data, violates the FCRA, you may sue them in state or federal court.

Page 2 of 2

The FCRA gives several different federal agencies authority to enforce the FCRA:

For questions or concerns regarding	Please contact
CRAs, creditors and others not listed below	Federal Trade Commission Consumer Response Center- FCRA Washington, DC 20580 * 202-326-3761
National banks, federal branches/agencies of foreign banks (word "National" or initials "N.A." appear in or after bank's name)	Office of the Comptroller of the Currency Compliance Management, Mail Stop 6-6 Washington, DC 20219 * 800-613-6743
Federal Reserve System member banks (except national banks, and federal branches/agencies of foreign banks)	Federal Reserve Board Division of Consumer & Community Affairs Washington, DC 20551 * 202-452-3693
Savings associations and federally chartered savings banks (word "Federal" or initials "F.S.B." appear in federal institution's name)	Office of Thrift Supervision Consumer Programs Washington D.C. 20552* 800- 842-6929
Federal credit unions (words "Federal Credit Union" appear in institution's name)	National Credit Union Administration 1775 Duke Street Alexandria, VA 22314 * 703-518-6360
State-chartered banks that are not members of the Federal Reserve System	Federal Deposit Insurance Corporation Division of Compliance & Consumer Affairs Washington, DC 20429 * 800-934-FDIC
Air, surface, or rail common carriers regulated by former Civil Aeronautics Board or Interstate Commerce Commission	Department of Transportation Office of Financial Management Washington, DC 20590 * 202-366-1306
Activities subject to the Packers and Stockyards Act, 1921	Department of Agriculture Office of Deputy Administrator-GIPSA Washington, DC 20250 * 202-720-7051

Let's suppose you run the credit report and it comes back bad. You are convinced that if you hire this candidate you will be the target of theft and embezzlement. What do you do? Consider that in this day of identity theft, it is possible that the candidate's identity was stolen by someone else. It is also possible that someone at the credit reporting company typed in the wrong social security number and the information is inaccurate.

You need to put the candidate on notice that they are not being hired due to the credit report and give them the opportunity to review and dispute the report. Here is a sample letter:

Exhibit: Poor Credit No Hire Letter

\<Enter Date\>

Dear **\<Enter Candidate's Name\>**:

This letter is to notify you that we have obtained a copy of your consumer report for use in evaluating issues related to your potential employment. A copy of that report is attached and consists of information received from the following Consumer Reporting Agency(ies):

\<Enter Consumer Reporting Agency Name\>
\<Enter Consumer Reporting Agency Address\>
\<Enter Consumer Reporting Agency Phone Number\>

If any of the information contained in the report is incomplete or inaccurate, you may dispute the matter directly with the agency that provided the information by writing or calling the agency.

Based upon the information in our possession, we will be unable to offer you employment at this time. If you feel the information in our possession is incomplete or inaccurate please advise us within the next seven days.

Good luck in your job search.

Sincerely,

\<Enter Name\>

But what about criminal background checks? There are international, federal, state and county law enforcement organizations. How do you make sure you don't miss something? And do you really want to spend the time tracking down information? Probably not. Instead, hire the professional background verification company. And make sure they have adequate insurance.

Employee or Independent Contractor?

You've picked the perfect candidate and know they want the job. You know what you can afford to pay them. But should you pay them as a W-2 employee or a 1099 Independent Contractor? Many employers prefer to use independent contractors since they don't have to:

1. Withhold payroll taxes

2. Pay benefits

3. Match social security

4. Pay federal or state unemployment

Just having an agreement with the individual is not enough to determine status and a review of court cases indicates that the distinction between the two is not always clear. However, as an employer, the responsibility for using the correct classification falls on the agency owner.

Assume the individual is really an independent contractor but the agency chooses to pay him as an employee and provide employee benefits. The agency will bear the unnecessary extra cost of taxes paid and benefits provided.

On the other hand, assume the individual is really an employee but is paid as an independent contractor. The agency may be required to pay overdue taxes, issue retroactive W-2 forms, and provide retroactive medical, pension, and retirement benefits. Obviously, making the wrong decision can be an expensive mistake.

The issue of misclassification can arise in one of two ways. A worker who is treated as an independent contractor could go to the Department of Labor with a claim, or the Internal Revenue Service might decide to do a compliance audit to make sure the employer is in compliance regarding withholding and tax obligations.

A general rule is that you, the agency owner, have the *right to control or direct only the result of the work done* by an independent contractor, and *not the means and methods of accomplishing the result*. For more information, contact your Certified Public Account and/or visit www.irs.gov.

Making the Offer

Assume the person is categorized as an employee. Now is a good time to draft an employment offer letter. This letter should outline:

1. Position – What position is this person being hired for?

2. Compensation – How much is the person going to be paid and when is payday?

3. Start Date – When do you want the new employee to start?

4. Requirements – Do you expect the employee to satisfy any requirements (insurance license, drug testing, etc.)?

5. Candidate's Response – Require the candidate to accept or reject the offer.

Once a candidate has accepted an offer, you should also notify any other candidates that you have made an offer to someone else and that the offer was accepted. Below is a sample employment offer letter as well as a position filled letter.

Exhibit: Employment Offer Letter

\<Enter Date\>

Dear _____:

On behalf of **\<Enter Agency Name\>**, I am pleased to offer you a position as _____. Your annual compensation will be _____ and will be paid in equal semi-monthly installments on the 15th and last day of each month. You will report to _____ and we would like you to start work on _____.

The position for which you are being hired requires that you have or obtain a _____ license within sixty days of employment. Costs associated with any review or preparatory course will be reimbursed by **\<Enter Agency Name\>** only after you have successfully obtained the license. Should you not obtain this license within sixty days of employment your employment will be terminated.

This offer is contingent upon the results of your: reference / background check, motor vehicle report (MVR), credit report, drug screening and physical examination.

To complete the drug screening and physical examination please make an appointment with _____ _____ by calling _____. The screening and exam must be completed at least ten (10) days prior to the commencement of your employment. Your employment is also contingent upon you completing, signing and returning the attached Non-Piracy Agreement on your first day of work.

We look forward to hearing from you about this offer. Please indicate your acceptance of this offer by signing below and returning a copy of this letter with your original signature to me no later than _____.

Sincerely,

\<Enter Name & Title\>

I ☐ accept ☐ do not accept **\<Enter Agency Name\>** offer of employment. I understand that my employment is considered "at will," and that either \<Enter Agency Name\> or I may terminate this employment relationship at any time with or without cause or notice.

_____   _____
Signature   Date

Exhibit: Position Filled Letter

<Enter Date>

Dear _____:

I would like to take this opportunity to thank you for taking the time to speak with me regarding our need for a _____ and appreciate your patience throughout our search process.

While we were very impressed with your qualifications, we were faced with a difficult decision. We have finally selected another candidate who we believe more closely fits what we are looking for in this position.

We will keep your resume on file should we become aware of any other appropriate positions in the near future.

Thank you again for your interest and good luck in your future endeavors.

Sincerely,
<Enter Name & Title>

First Day of Work

Your new employee shows up for the first day of work. What do you do with your new employee? Obviously there are a number of administrative functions that should be part of the orientation process.

Start off by making a Personnel Folder for the employee. You should immediately include all the information previously gathered on the employee. This would include the: resume, application, MVR authorization, FCRA authorization, etc.

You are also going to need to provide the candidate with a copy of the employee handbook, his or her job description, and any sort of non-piracy / employment agreement you expect them to sign. As you distribute each of these you should get written acknowledgement for each one.

Keys to the office, computer passwords, and all the forms related to payroll and employee benefits should be distributed, completed, and collected. Having a standard New Employee Checklist can be very helpful to make sure you don't miss, skip, or ignore something.

You should also collect emergency contact information for the employee in case an accident or illness occurs at work. Due to the confidential nature of this information, it should be kept in a separate file in a secured location accessible to only a limited number of management.

Exhibit: New Employee Checklist

New Employee Checklist for _____

Employee Signature _____ Date _____

Pre-Employment	Completed?	Mgr. Initials
Application filled out & signed?	❑ Yes ❑ No	
Signed background check authorization?	❑ Yes ❑ No	
Signed drug testing authorization?	❑ Yes ❑ No	
Signed MVR authorization?	❑ Yes ❑ No	
Signed credit check authorization?	❑ Yes ❑ No	
Proof of Valid Insurance License?	❑ Yes ❑ No	
Proof of Valid Driver's License?	❑ Yes ❑ No	
Drug testing results reviewed?	❑ Yes ❑ No	
Criminal Background check completed?	❑ Yes ❑ No	
MVR reviewed?	❑ Yes ❑ No	
References		
References verified and contacted?	❑ Yes ❑ No	
Previous employment verified and contacted?	❑ Yes ❑ No	
Signature Acknowledgements		
Employee Handbook	❑ Yes ❑ No	
Job Description	❑ Yes ❑ No	
Non-Piracy / Employment Agreement	❑ Yes ❑ No	
General		
Employment file created?	❑ Yes ❑ No	
Key(s) to office distributed?	❑ Yes ❑ No	
Computer passwords assigned?	❑ Yes ❑ No	
Direct Deposit forms provided?	❑ Yes ❑ No	
Entered into payroll system?	❑ Yes ❑ No	
Voice mail set up?	❑ Yes ❑ No	
Supervisor given record of employee's computer, email, and voicemail passwords?	❑ Yes ❑ No	

Government Required	Completed?	Mgr. Initials
Employment Eligibility Verification Form (I-9)	❑ Yes ❑ No	
Federal Tax Withholding Form (W-4)	❑ Yes ❑ No	
State Tax Withholding Form	❑ Yes ❑ NA	
Local Tax Withholding Form	❑ Yes ❑ NA	

Page 1 of 2

New Employee Checklist for _____

Employee Signature _____ Date _____

Employee Benefits Enrollment	Completed?	Employee's Initials
Healthcare	❑ Yes ❑ No	
Disability	❑ Yes ❑ No	
Vision	❑ Yes ❑ No	
Dental	❑ Yes ❑ No	
Life Insurance	❑ Yes ❑ No	
Pension / 401(k)	❑ Yes ❑ No	
Section 125 Cafeteria Plan	❑ Yes ❑ No	

Emergency Contact Form

Employee Information

Name	Social Security Number
Home Address	Home Phone
Date of Birth	Cell Phone

In Case of an Emergency Primary Contact

Name	Relationship
Home Address	Home Phone
Work Phone	Cell Phone

Secondary Contact

Name	Relationship
Home Address	Home Phone
Work Phone	Cell Phone

Physician Information (optional)

Name	
Office Address	Office Phone
Home Phone	Cell Phone

Known Allergies or Medical Conditions (optional)

You are not required to provide any information in this section, but if you want us to have information that may help us in a medical emergency (and for no other purpose) you are invited to voluntarily disclose such information.

_____

_____

Page 2 of 2

Non-Piracy and Non-Compete Agreements

One of the most frequently asked questions is, "Where can I find some good producers?" If you want good, experienced producers, you are not going to hire them right out of college. They might come from another industry, but like the recent graduate, it will take time for them to develop a significant book of business.

Obviously, the best place to find producers is from your competitors. Unfortunately for the hirer, most agencies have had their producers sign non-piracy or non-compete agreements.

Slightly over 42 percent of respondents surveyed for *Maximizing Agency Value II: A Guide for Buying, Selling, and Perpetuating Insurance Agencies* indicated that the producers of agencies they purchased had either a non-piracy or non-compete agreement. While these documents have varying degrees of enforceability, depending upon how they are structured and state law, it is an obstacle to the hiring agency.

A non-piracy agreement is specific in terms of time and clientele. It prevents a former employee from writing or attempting to write his former accounts for a specific period of time.

A non-compete agreement is specific in terms of time and geographic scope. It is more restrictive in that it prevents the former employee from working in an agency within a specific geographic area or distance from his former agency. While non-compete agreements are more restrictive, they are more difficult to enforce in a court of law. The exception to this is when the Seller of an agency signs a non-compete agreement. This is generally found to be enforceable.

As a result, highly compensated producers are reluctant to move. They want to maintain their high level of compensation, but may not immediately bring a significant book of business with them. This could result in negative cash flow for the hiring agency.

As you interview candidates, you should ask if they have an employment agreement (non-compete or non-piracy) and review it. And while you are interviewing the candidate you should make reference to any requirement you have for them to sign a non-piracy agreement. Non-producer candidates may have signed a non-piracy agreement with their former employer, but you usually want to hire them for their technical skills, not so they can solicit clients.

On the following pages is a sample Non-Piracy Agreement. This sample Non-Piracy Agreement can be converted into a Non-Compete Agreement by changing the name of the agreement and substituting Paragraph 9 with the following:

Competition. The Employee agrees that during his or her employment and for a period of three (3) years after leaving the employment of the Corporation, he or she will not directly or indirectly, solicit, attempt to obtain, accept or in any fashion engage in the property and casualty insurance business (including that of a property and casualty insurance agent, broker, advisor, consultant or risk manager) within twenty-five (25) miles of **<STREET ADDRESS>**.

Exhibit: Employment and Non-Piracy Agreement

EMPLOYMENT AND NON-PIRACY AGREEMENT

This Agreement entered into this _____ day of _____ , 20_____ , by and between **<AGENCY>**, a **<STATE>** corporation, hereinafter referred to as "the Corporation" and **<Name of Employee>**, hereinafter referred to as "the Employee".

1. **Purpose.** The purpose of this Agreement is to set forth some of the terms and parameters of employment relating to the Corporation's business. These terms of employment shall be in addition to the terms set forth in any employee handbook, personnel policy statement, or similar expression of policy issued by the Corporation, as amended by the Corporation from time to time, and in addition to compensation separately agreed upon. If there should be a conflict between the terms of this Agreement and the terms of the handbook or policy, this Agreement shall be controlling.

2. **Consideration.** The consideration for this Agreement is the compensation which is actually paid the Employee by the Corporation.

3. **Status of Parties.** The Employee acknowledges that his or her relationship with the Corporation is that of employer and employee.

4. **Other Employment.** The Employee shall devote all of his or her working time to the business of the Corporation and shall not, during the term of this Agreement, accept similar employment nor perform independent services for other entities, whether or not such entities are in competition with the Corporation, without obtaining written permission from the Corporation.

5. **Property of the Corporation.** All insurance business, including renewals, whether property, casualty, life or other, produced by the Employee during the continuation of this Agreement shall be written through the Corporation and if brokered elsewhere, it shall be done only in the name of the Corporation and only with the Corporation's written consent. All business produced by the Employee or worked on by the Employee may be coded or otherwise identified to indicate its source of production, however, notwithstanding such identification, all such business including the expiration data and all files and records in connection therewith, shall be the exclusive property of the Corporation and shall continue to be so after the termination of this Agreement for whatever cause, and the Employee hereby waives and releases all claims of right or ownership thereto and covenants that he shall not make or retain copies of such property by computer record or otherwise.

6. **Billing, Correspondence, and Advertising.** All premiums shall be billed by and shall be owed to the Corporation, all checks and drafts in payment of such premiums shall be made payable to the Corporation, and all money received in payment of premiums or other fees shall be turned over to the Corporation in the form received and deposited in the Corporation's account. All correspondence and all publicity and advertising shall be carried on in the Corporation's name.

Page 1 of 3

7. **Deductions From Compensation.** All taxes and other deductions required by law shall be made from the Employee's compensation. Any overpayment of compensation, whether resulting from miscalculation or otherwise, shall be deducted from the Employee's future compensation. The Employee agrees that he or she shall be indebted to the Corporation for any excess commissions paid to him or her as the result of the subsequent cancellation of a policy, and that he or she shall be indebted to the Corporation in the amount of any premiums which the Corporation is required to pay an insurance company as the result of the Employee's failure to timely cancel a policy sold by him or her due to non-payment of premiums to the Corporation by the customer. The Employee further agrees that any sums owed by him or her to the Corporation and the value of any property of the Corporation in his or her possession at the time of termination of employment are advances of wages which the Employee authorizes be deducted from any future compensation to which the Employee may be due from the Corporation.

8. **Confidentiality.** The Employee recognizes and agrees that the Corporation's business is highly competitive and that in the course of it he or she will become acquainted with confidential information belonging to the Corporation which is valuable, specialized, and a unique asset of the Corporation. This information relates to persons, firms and corporations which are or may become customers or accounts of the Corporation during the term of this Agreement, and sources with which insurance is placed including, but not limited to, the names of customers, policy expiration dates, policy terms, conditions and rates, familiarity with customers' risk characteristics, and information concerning the insurance markets for large or unusual commercial risks. The Employee agrees that he or she will not without the written consent of the Corporation disclose or make any use of any such confidential information, except as may be required in the course of his or her employment hereunder during the course of his or her employment with the Corporation or at any time after the termination of the employment.

9. **Non-Piracy.** The Employee agrees that during his or her employment and for a period of three (3) years after leaving the employment of the Corporation, he or she will not engage directly or indirectly in competition with the Corporation by directly or indirectly soliciting or accepting insurance or bond business from or performing any of the services performed by the Corporation for any customer of the Corporation or any potential customer of the Corporation being solicited for business by the Corporation at the time of the termination of employment regardless of the location of such specific customer and regardless of the place of work of the Employee.

10. **Injunctive Relief.** In the event of a breach or threatened breach by the Employee of the provisions of paragraph 8 or 9 hereof, the Corporation shall be entitled to a temporary restraining order, temporary injunction and permanent injunction restraining the Employee from such activity. In the event of litigation, the prevailing party shall be entitled to recover from the non-prevailing party all costs incurred, including reasonable attorney's fees in enforcing the provisions of this Agreement. Nothing herein shall be construed as prohibiting either party from pursuing any other rights or remedies at law or in equity available for such breach or threatened breach of the provisions of this Agreement, including the recovery of damages, and all such rights and remedies shall be cumulative.

11. Certain Commissions and Fees. In addition to injunctive relief as provided for herein, if any commission or fees become payable to the Employee or to any person, firm, or corporation by whom the Employee has been employed or affiliated or in which the Employee has had an interest whether direct or indirect, as a result of a violation by the Employee of the provisions of paragraph 8 or 9 of this Agreement, the Employee agrees to pay promptly to the Corporation an amount equal to one hundred percent (100%) of such commissions or fees or the commissions or fees last charged by the Corporation to such customer, whichever is higher, for three (3) years beginning with the first date that such commissions or fees became payable to such other person, notwithstanding the fact that such period of damages may be longer than the period of non-competition provided in paragraph 9 above. These commissions and fees shall be the sole damages to which the Corporation shall be entitled in the event of a breach by the Employee of the provisions of paragraph 9 of this Agreement and the parties recognize that in the event of such a breach the Corporation's damages would not be limited to a single year's lost commissions or fees. If the Corporation must institute suit in order to collect these damages, it shall be entitled to recover its reasonable attorneys' fees from the Employee.

12. Severability. The provisions of this Agreement shall be severable, and if any provision of this agreement shall be unenforceable or invalid, then the remainder of the provisions of this Agreement shall not be affected thereby. If any of the restrictions of this Agreement shall be unenforceable, they are for too long a period or cover too broad a geographical area, or for any reason whatsoever, it is agreed that the restrictions shall be effective for such a period of time and for such area and to such extent as the same may be enforceable.

13. Assignment and Successorship. In the event of the sale, merger, other acquisition or reorganization of the Corporation into some form of business other than a corporation, this Agreement shall be assignable to the successor entity.

14. Jurisdiction and Venue. This Agreement shall in all respects be interpreted, construed, and given effect according to the laws of the State of <STATE>. Jurisdiction to enforce this Agreement shall lie in <STATE> and venue shall be proper in any county where the Corporation maintains an office.

15. Termination. This Agreement may be terminated by notice of either Employee or the Corporation furnished to the other, at any time hereafter. Termination of the Agreement shall only affect employment and shall have no effect whatsoever on the remaining provisions of this agreement.

WITNESS our hands and seals this _____ day of _____, 20__.

WITNESSES: **<AGENCY>**

_____   _____
                                          As to Corporation   President

_____   _____
                                          As to Employee   Employee

You should note that you can require new employees to sign a non-piracy agreement as a stipulation to accepting the position. However, you cannot require existing employees to sign such an agreement.

If you ask an existing employee to sign it and he does, it is not enforceable since there was no consideration given to the employee. If you tell an existing employee to sign the agreement if he wants to keep his job, it's not enforceable even if he signs it since it was signed under duress.

So how do you get existing employees to sign it? Well, you could pay them to sign it, but what is "adequate consideration?" It's another one of those wonderful legal terms that is not clearly defined and won't be until you are in the courtroom. If you are truly promoting an existing employee, say from personal lines CSR to office manager, you can require a signed non-piracy agreement as part of the promotion.

Enforceability of restrictive covenants varies greatly on a state by state basis. Some states, including Texas and California, have very specific requirements to make an agreement enforceable. <u>Before using a non-piracy or non-compete agreement, make sure you have consulted with an employment law attorney in your state as to its form and enforceability.</u>

Evaluations

Evaluations are the means by which the agency can determine if it is making optimal use of an agency's human resources. Is it wisely managing its personnel? Do the employees know if they are achieving the levels of performance that management expects?

Employees want to know if management is happy or unhappy with their work, yet many managers avoid or delay evaluations because they feel evaluations are confrontational and that they need to result in a compensation increase. This is a perception that needs to be dispelled.

It should be reinforced with managers and employees that evaluations are a positive influence on both the agency and the employee. Proper evaluations should show employees:

1. How they are doing and what additional steps can be taken to increase their value to the agency.

2. What they can do to enhance their job security.

3. What they can do to achieve increased compensation.

4. How they fit into the agency's goals.

5. What they can do in regards to their professional growth and development.

How often should evaluations be done? At least once a year, and more often for employees in a new position. And just because someone is being reviewed does not mean it has to be associated with an increase in compensation.

Managers need to perform regular audits of employees' work and provide constructive feedback on a regular basis. The performance review should not be a time to air issues that have been "building up." There should be no surprises to the employee if the manager has provided regular comments as to their work and what areas of concern might exist.

Reviews should be looked upon as a sharing of information and perceptions as well as developing personal action plans for the future. You may want to consider having the employee review himself/herself prior to meeting with you. Then the evaluator and the evaluatee share their thoughts with each other. Typically, the person being evaluated is harder on himself than the evaluator.

Plan your evaluations. As a manager, you should mark on your calendar the date when each of your subordinates is due to be evaluated. Make it part of your "To Do" list and actively manage the process. One of the worst things a manager can do is "forget" to do an evaluation and wait until the employee comes in and asks to be evaluated.

Evaluations can and should be tailored to the job description. Unfortunately most managers use "off-the-shelf" evaluations that address an employee's traits but not the specific functions of the position.

A good evaluation form should have five components:

1) **Achievement of Objectives Section** – Did the employee achieve the major functions of the specific job he or she is in? Were the standards achieved? For example: If the receptionist job description says, "Answers the telephone within three rings in a professional manner," did the receptionist do this on a consistent basis?

   Obviously, an evaluation like this needs to be tied into job descriptions (See section 4 of this book.) The following sample evaluation form's achievement of objectives section has an area for:

   a) The job function number – This would be the function number from the job description.

   b) Weight – The sample form has room to evaluate five job functions. You can increase or decrease this accordingly but you should include the major functions. Note that the weights in this section must total 100 percent.

   c) Score – This sample form is based on a scale of one to ten with ten being the best and one being the worst.

d) Comments – Any specific comments, positive or negative, regarding the performance of this function should go here.

A word of caution; if you have five personal lines CSRs in your agency, a) and b) above should be identical for all of them. If they are not identical, it could be argued that you are not treating them equally and you are being discriminatory.

If people are performing the same job, you'd better have a very good reason why you are evaluating them on different tasks. Obviously, different positions could and should have different function numbers and weights.

2) **Traits Section** – What are the general traits you want in an employee? Professionalism, good attendance, appearance, problem-solving skills? This section is where you list these traits. Like the achievement of objectives section, they should be weighted totaling 100% and be scored on a scale of one to ten. To simplify the evaluation process, select traits that you want everyone in your agency to possess.

3) **Development Plan Section** – At the beginning of each year you should sit down with the employee and discuss his or her development plan. This could include educational goals (CIC, CISR, etc.), attaining a designation, or learning some new responsibilities within the agency. Include the details in the "Plan for coming year" area of the Development Plan.

When the employee is being evaluated at the end of the year, comments of how well the person achieved the development plan should be included in the appropriate section. Like the two previous sections, develop a score (1 to 10) on how well this person has developed.

4) **Comments Section** – Any additional comments the reviewer has that was not included elsewhere in the evaluation should go here. The section should also have an area for the employee to provide any comments or responses.

5) **Scorecard** – Here is where you quantify the evaluation. All the weights and scores from the Achievement of Objectives and Traits sections get copied over and extended (weight times score) to develop an average for each of these two sections.

The total of the weights for the Achievement of Objectives must total 100% but do not have to be equal. For example: If you have five objectives, you can weight each of them at 20% or the first two at 35% and the remaining three at 10%. The weighting is totally up to you based on what you feel is important to job achievement.

Likewise, the weights in the Traits section must total 100% but do not have to be equal. Use your discretion on what is important.

Once you have a weighted average for the Achievement of Objectives and Traits section, transfer them to the Weighted Average Section. You should also input the score for the Development Plan here. Then input the relative weights for the three sections. While the combined weights must again total 100%, it is up to you as to how to allocate the percentages between Achievement of Objectives, Traits, and Development Plan.

Before you can do an evaluation of this type, you must be prepared. At the beginning of the evaluation period, the manager must select the major job functions to be evaluated as well as the weights for this section, the traits section, and the weighted average section. This information needs to be shared with the employee and together they should agree upon a development plan. Once these details are finalized, both the supervisor and the employee should retain a copy until the year-end evaluation is done.

Exhibit: Employee Evaluation

<INSERT AGENCY NAME>

Employee Evaluation

Employee Name: _____

Employee Position: _____

For the Period: _____ to _____

The employee's signature below indicates neither agreement nor disagreement with the following evaluation. It does indicate that this evaluation has been reviewed and discussed with the employee on the date indicated.

_____   _____

Employee's Signature   Date

_____   _____

Supervisor's Signature   Date

Section 1 - Achievement of Objectives

1) Job Function # ____	Weight ____	Score ____	Comments_____ _____
2) Job Function # ____	Weight ____	Score ____	Comments_____ _____
3) Job Function # ____	Weight ____	Score ____	Comments_____ _____
4) Job Function # ____	Weight ____	Score ____	Comments_____ _____
5) Job Function # ____	Weight ____	Score ____	Comments_____ _____

Page 1 of 4

Section 2 - Traits

Traits	Weight	Score	Comments
Courteousness			
Professionalism			
Friendliness			
Calm & In Control			
Attendance			
Appearance			
Quality of Work			
Quantity of Work			
Problem Solving			
Communication Skills			
Weight must total 100%			

Section 3 – Development Plan

Plan for coming year

Comments on achievement of plan

Development Plan Score _____

Section 4 – Comments

Manager's concluding comments

Employee's Response

Page 3 of 4

Scorecard

Achievement of Objectives	Weight	Score	Extension (Weight x Score)
1)			
2)			
3)			
4)			
5)			
The above percentages must total	100%	Total	(a)

Traits	Weight	Score	Extension (Weight x Score)
Courteousness			
Professionalism			
Friendly			
Calm			
Attendance			
Appearance			
Quality of Work			
Quantity of Work			
Problem Solving			
Communication			
The above percentages must total	100%	Total	(b)

Weighted Average	Weight	Score	Extension (Weight x Score)
Achievement of Objectives		(a)	
Traits		(b)	
Development Plan			
The above percentages must total	100%	Final Score	

Final Score

9.00 – 10.00	Outstanding
8.00 – 8.99	Above Average
7.00 – 7.99	Average
6.00 – 6.99	Below Average
Less than 6.00	Unacceptable

Training & Development

You've spent a lot of time and money to hire the "right" candidate. Now you have got to make sure that you develop your employee's talents. If you pigeonhole them into a dead-end position, chances are that they will eventually leave and then you have to start the recruiting process all over again.

Training can emanate from two areas, internal and external. Internally, the agency should consider cross-training employees to ensure adequate backup when someone is absent. This will help to maintain quality client service. If your agency is large enough, you might also consider in-house training and web-based training.

From an external standpoint, the agency should encourage employees to attend association programs, take applicable college courses, and work towards an industry recognized designation such as those offered by the National Alliance. Additional information about the National Alliance can be found at their website:

www.TheNationalAlliance.com

To make sure the employees of the agency are taking the appropriate development courses, the agency needs to assign training and professional development responsibility to one person who will focus on it. Otherwise, there is a potential for misuse of employee time and excessive costs.

Involuntary Termination

Terminating an employee is one of the most difficult decisions a manager has to make. Why should an employee be terminated? It could be that their performance is not meeting expectations. But have those performance standards been communicated? If you have job descriptions and you do performance evaluations like the one earlier in this section, those standards have probably been communicated.

Is it a behavioral problem? Your employee is rude to customers and cannot get along with his fellow employees. Or there could be a personal problem that has impacted his job performance. Whatever the case, you need to be prepared for the termination process if you hope to reduce potential lawsuits.

Any attorney will tell you that the first step in the termination process is developing a paper trail. It should outline what performance has been unacceptable and what you have done to correct the situation. In some instances an event is so egregious that you are justified in terminating an employee immediately. But most terminations are due to poor performance and occur over a period of time.

Is your paper trail adequate? Only an attorney can tell you that, but you should document everything. Even if you are orally reprimanding an employee, you need to document it.

You should develop a Corrective Action Form that can be used for written or oral reprimands. It should indicate the time and date of the reprimand as well as whether it was done in writing or verbally. Be as specific as possible regarding the reason for the reprimand and list only facts, not opinions. Whenever possible give concrete examples.

But what is the desired result of this action? What do you expect? State what the employee should do to improve performance. When available, you should refer back to the agency handbook or job description, both for which the employee should have signed.

You should also indicate when this issue will be reviewed again. Like employee evaluations, the manager issuing the corrective action should mark on his calendar when this issue is due for review. "Forgetting" to review the corrective action could result in an assumption that it has been corrected and no further action is necessary.

If the corrective action is in writing, make sure the employee signs the form to indicate that the issue has been discussed with her. These forms should also be taken into consideration when doing an employee's performance appraisal. You shouldn't issue a reprimand one week and then give a positive performance review the following week, along with a raise. Inconsistency can kill you in the courtroom.

Exhibit: Corrective Action Form

Corrective Action Form

Employee _____	Reprimand Date _____
Reprimand was: ❏ Oral ❏ Written	Reprimand Time _____

Reason for Reprimand:

_____

_____

_____

Corrective Action Required of Employee:

_____

_____

_____

Corrective action will be reviewed in _____ days.

Employee's Signature

(Not required for oral reprimand)

Manager's Signature

If you decide it is in the best interest of the agency to terminate an employee, you should have clear guidelines on how to handle the termination. You need to be consistent and have a specific procedure for the termination meeting, return of agency property, final pay and benefit continuation.

The first step in terminating an employee is to review the situation with the other owners or appropriate managers in the agency. Make sure you maintain confidentiality. You don't want an employee to find out he is being terminated from a fellow employee an hour before you hold the termination meeting.

Talk to an employment law attorney to verify that your paper trail is sufficient to clearly document that the performance or conduct is unacceptable and that you gave the employee adequate opportunity to take corrective action. The attorney should also verify that you are not violating any Federal, State or Local employment laws.

You should then write a termination letter that states the specific reason the employee is being terminated. While employment is "at will" and you don't need a reason to terminate an employee, having a specific reason can stop a disgruntled employee from arguing that he was unfairly discharged.

The termination letter should also address end dates of benefits and conversion options and process, if available. You may want to give the employee the letter during or immediately after the termination meeting, but since you won't be sending it by certified mail, you should obtain some other documentation from the employee that he received it.

When an employee terminates, he may be eligible to continue his health insurance coverage under COBRA. (See page 63.) Due to the critical nature of handling COBRA rights properly, many employers engage outside service providers to assist them with their COBRA compliance efforts. Although these firms can provide invaluable assistance to employers, the primary responsibility for COBRA compliance rests with the employer.

Therefore, it is critical for employers to coordinate their COBRA compliance efforts carefully with their COBRA services, health insurance carriers, or Third Party Administrators to ensure that there is a clear understanding of all of the various COBRA notice rules and the party who will be responsible for compliance with each of those rules.

Exhibit: Termination Letter

<Enter Date>

<Enter Employee Name>
<Enter Employee Street Address>
<Enter Employee City, State, Zip>

Dear <Enter Employee Name>:
This letter serves as a confirmation of our discussion, in which you were notified that your employment with <Enter Agency Name> is being terminated. The reason for this termination is **<Enter Reason>**. Your last day of employment with this organization will be <Enter Date>. As a terminating employee, there are a number of issues related to your benefits of which you will need to be aware.

Final Pay
You will be paid your regular compensation through **<Enter Date>**. Paychecks will be mailed to you (or direct deposited if applicable) on the regularly scheduled paydays.

Medical and Dental Coverage
You have the option to continue your group medical and dental coverage through the COBRA Plan. All agency paid benefits cease on **<Enter Appropriate Date>**. Information will be sent to you shortly by certified mail regarding your options to elect COBRA coverage.

Group Term Life Insurance
Your coverage ceases on your termination date; however, you have the option to convert your group term life insurance to an individual policy with **<Enter Name of Carrier>** within ___ days following your termination date. If you are interested, please contact the carrier directly to obtain a conversion form.

Flexible Spending Account
If you have a balance in your flexible spending account when you terminate employment, you may continue to file claims for eligible expenses against the balance until the end of the plan year, **<Enter date plan year ends>**.

401(k) Plan
If you have participated in the 401(k) Plan, you can roll over your investment to an Individual Retirement Account (IRA) should you so desire. Please contact your personal financial advisor to assist you in this matter.

To insure you receive documents and notices from the agency, be sure to contact us if your address changes. Please call me should you have any questions.

Sincerely yours,

<Enter Name and Title>

After preparing the termination letter, it is time to have a termination meeting. It is always advisable to have a third person in the meeting as a witness. You don't want an employee to say you offered to not terminate her if she would have sex with you.

The meeting should be in private, towards the end of the day, so that it is less disruptive to the office. Get right to the point; this is a termination, not a discussion or negotiation. You should be specific as to why the termination is taking place and what the employee is entitled to in regards to pay and benefits.

When the employee is cleaning out his or her desk, make sure that you have someone stay with them to ensure they do not take property that doesn't belong to them. Just like on their first day of work, it's helpful to have a termination checklist. You may want to include as part of the termination checklist questions regarding reference information.

Voluntary Termination

Sometimes an employee resigns due to retirement, accepting a position with another company, or a desire to relocate. In these situations an exit interview should occur. Some of the questions that should be posed to the departing employee include:

1. What is your reason for leaving the agency?

2. What did you like about the agency?

3. What did you dislike about the agency?

4. What recommendations would you make to improve or enhance the agency?

5. Would you recommend the agency to others as a place to work?

The exit interview should be handled by someone other than the immediate supervisor of the departing employee. This will provide the employee with the ability to be forthright about any problems with his or her supervisor.

Make sure that you discuss when benefits end and the conversion options (if any). Don't forget about COBRA! Voluntarily terminating employees are also eligible to continue health insurance coverage under COBRA, assuming they qualify. (See the information on COBRA under Section 2: Employment Law).

The termination checklist on the next page can be used for both voluntarily and involuntarily terminating employees.

Exhibit: Termination Checklist

Termination Checklist for _____

Effective date of termination _____

Return of:		Employee Initials
Employee Handbook	❒ Yes ❒ No	
Key(s) to office	❒ Yes ❒ No	
Laptop & other automation equipment	❒ Yes ❒ No	
All client files and information	❒ Yes ❒ No	
All carrier files and information	❒ Yes ❒ No	
All other confidential information	❒ Yes ❒ No	
Notification:		
Has employee been given termination letter?	❒ Yes ❒ No	
Has COBRA Notification Letter been given / sent to employee?	❒ Yes ❒ No	
Computer Access:		
Has computer password been deactivated?	❒ Yes ❒ No	
Have all on-line company passwords been changed?	❒ Yes ❒ No	
References: (May we provide future potential employers or their representatives)		
Your start date?	❒ Yes ❒ No	
Your termination date?	❒ Yes ❒ No	
Your compensation history?	❒ Yes ❒ No	
Your position history?	❒ Yes ❒ No	
The reason for your termination?	❒ Yes ❒ No	

Employee's Signature _____   Date _____

Manager's Signature _____   Date _____

Section 2: Employment Law

Introduction to Employment Law

The previous section of this book addressed hiring, firing, and the interview process. And all states except Montana are employment at will states. But what does this mean? Can you fire anyone you want at any time? No.

The employment-at-will concept allows employers to terminate employees at any time, for any legal reason, or for no reason at all. Conversely, an employee can quit at any time, for any reason, without giving notice. In general the courts have upheld the right to terminate at will, but to help avoid discrimination claims, employers should follow their normal termination procedures whenever possible. The at-will clause should only be used to give you flexibility in your employment decisions.

However, "at-will" doesn't give employers free reign to terminate employees for no reason. The courts have restricted the at-will relationship under several legal theories. For example:

- The termination violated some public policy.

- The termination violated a "whistleblower" statute.

- The employer's action constituted a wrongful act.

Another reason for caution is that many employees are specially protected under federal, state, or local discrimination laws, which must be complied with regardless of at-will status. If you terminate a protected employee for no reason or without following your normal disciplinary process, you are raising a red flag and may be provoking a challenge to the termination. And many of these discrimination laws apply to the hiring and promotion phases of employment, not just the termination phase.

This section of Managing Human Resources in an Insurance Agency addresses many of the Federal laws employers must comply with. Please realize that a state or local municipality can make a Federal law more encompassing (i.e. more restrictive) but not less encompassing.

For example: Title VII of the Federal Civil Rights Act is the law that prevents discrimination against race, color, sex, religion, and national origin. But in California it's race, color, sex, religion, national origin, sexual orientation, and marital status.

Most states have their own non-discrimination/fair employment laws, which are modeled after Federal laws. But be careful, many states have made their laws more restrictive, thereby offering greater protection.

The following is a general overview of some of the more important Federal employment laws that can impact insurance agencies. This section is by no means exhaustive, and laws do change from time to time. Before acting on any human resource issue that has governing law, check with an employment law attorney to make sure that you are in compliance with all applicable employment laws.

Throughout this section are website references for additional information on the specific Federal law. In general, significant information can be found at the Department of Labor Website (www.dol.gov) and the Equal Employment Opportunity Commission website (www.eeoc.gov).

Fair Labor Standards Act

Year Enacted: 1938

Enforced by: Department of Labor, Wage and Hour Division

Applies to: Employers who engage in interstate commerce

The Fair Labor Standards Act (FLSA) establishes minimum wage, overtime pay, recordkeeping, and child labor standards affecting full-time and part-time workers. Overtime pay must be at a rate of at least one and one-half times their regular pay rate for hours worked in excess of 40 hours per week.

This law protects employees of companies who engage in interstate commerce. But just because your agency doesn't have any clients outside of your state, don't think this is your "get out of jail free" card. You use the mail and make long distance telephone calls. Your carriers are also located in other states. You affect interstate commerce.

This law exempts some employees from its overtime pay requirements. These employees are known as "exempt" employees. Employees who you are required to pay overtime to are know as "non-exempt" employees. Whether an employee is exempt or non-exempt has <u>nothing</u> to do with whether they are paid an hourly wage or a salary. Any hourly rate can be converted to an annual salary and vice versa.

Employers should check the exact terms and conditions as to who is and is not exempt from overtime by contacting their local Wage and Hour Division office. These offices are listed in most telephone directories under U.S. Government, Department of Labor, Wage and Hour Division. In general, agency employees are exempt if they meet one of the following qualifications:

1) Executive Exemption (Must meet all of the following)
    a. Compensated on a salary basis at a rate not less than $455 per week.
    b. Primary duty must be managing the agency or a customarily recognized department of the agency.
    c. Must regularly direct the work of at least two or more full-time employees or their equivalent.
    d. Must have the authority to hire or hire other employees.

2) Administrative Exemption (Must meet all of the following)
    a. Compensated on a salary basis at a rate not less than $455 per week.
    b. Primary duty must be the performance of office or non-manual work directly related to the management or general business operations of the employer or the employer's customers.
    c. Primary duty includes the exercise of discretion and independent judgment with respect to matters of significance.

3) Professional Exemption (Must meet all of the following)
    a. Compensated on a salary basis at a rate not less than $455 per week.
    b. Performance of work requiring advanced knowledge, predominantly intellectual in nature and which includes work requiring the consistent exercise of discretion and judgment.
    c. Advanced knowledge must be in a field of science or learning
    d. Advanced knowledge must be customarily acquired by a prolonged course of specialized intellectual instruction.

4) Outside Sales (Must meet all of the following)
    a. Primary duty is making sales or obtaining orders or contracts for services for which the client will pay a consideration.
    b. Must be customarily and regularly engaged away from the employer's place or places of business.

5) Highly Compensated Employees (Must meet all of the following)
    a. Salary level is at least $100,000/year
    b. Performs office or non-manual work
    c. Regularly performs any one or more of the exempt duties identified in the standard tests for executive, administrative or professional exemptions.

You will note that the salary basis of $455 per week does not apply to the outside sales exemption. But what exactly does the government mean by "salary basis?" In addition to their regular pay, salary includes commissions and non-discretionary bonuses. It also means that you cannot dock their pay. The employee:

1. Regularly receives a pre-determined amount of compensation each pay period.
2. Cannot be reduced because of variations in the quantity or quality of work.
3. Must be paid his full salary for any week in which the employee performed any work.
4. Need not be paid for <u>any</u> workweek when no work is performed.

There are seven exceptions for docking pay:

1. Absences for one or more full days for personal reasons other than sickness or disability.
2. Absences for one or more full days due to sickness or disability if deduction is made under a bona fide plan, policy, or practice of providing wage replacement benefits for these types of absences.
3. To offset any amounts received as payment for jury fees, witness fees, or military pay.
4. Penalties imposed in good faith for violating safety rules of "major significance."
5. Unpaid disciplinary suspension of one or more full days imposed in good faith for violations of workplace conduct rules.

6. Proportionate part of salary paid for time actually worked in the first and last weeks of employment.
7. Unpaid leave pursuant to the Family and Medical Leave Act.

The FLSA doesn't limit the number of hours in a day or the number of days in a week that an employee works, as long as the employee is at least 16 years old, nor does it limit the number of hours of overtime that may be scheduled.

It does, however require non-exempt employees to be paid at least one and one-half times their regular rates of pay for all hours worked in excess of 40 in a workweek. The operative word here it "worked." Assume a non-exempt employee is entitled to paid vacation. If an employee takes Monday as a vacation day and then works ten hours per day Tuesday through Friday, the employee should be paid straight time for 48 hours, not 40 hours at regular pay and eight hours at time and a half. This is because the employee only <u>worked</u> 40 hours that week. Vacation, sick leave, personal days, etc. are not considered time <u>worked</u>.

Now let's assume a disgruntled employee leaves, goes to the Department of Labor, and complains that you didn't pay overtime. One of the first things the DOL will ask the employee is for a record of his or her time. How convenient, the employee just so happened to have written down their start and end times each day in their day timer.

The Department of Labor then contacts you and asks for your attendance records. And what do they show? Whether a person worked that day or took vacation or sick leave. The records don't show the employee's start and end times. Guess what? You lose. Employers must keep records on wages, hours, and other information as set forth in the Department of Labor's regulations.

Does this mean you should install a time clock? Yes, but there are more professional ways to track time than requiring an employee to punch in and out. Let's assume you have a local area network in your agency. A recent Google search for the words "time clock" and "software" generated hundreds of hits.

These software programs run in the background of your network and track when an employee signs on and off the system. Your employee handbook should instruct employees to sign on to their computer as soon as they arrive in the office and are ready to begin work (but after they have eaten their Egg McMuffin.) It should also instruct them to sign off during lunch and when they leave at the end of the day. This way, the computer system can generate your detailed attendance records.

Many agency owners think they are protected from paying overtime by having a statement in their employee handbook saying that overtime must be pre-approved in writing. While this is a good statement to have in the handbook, it won't prevent you from losing an overtime lawsuit.

Assume Mary comes into the office early because she avoids heavy traffic and it gives her quiet time to get her desk cleaned up. You know this (or should know this) and if you don't pay her for these overtime hours you'll lose should Mary end up suing you. The reason is that you have been "unjustly enriched." Disagree? Ask Wal-Mart who has lost several cases where employees did extra work "off the clock."

Another situation is when an employee each lunch at her desk and continues to work and/or answers the phone. This time is not considered mealtime and should be included in hours worked when determining whether or not the employee has worked in excess of 40 hours.

What happens if you willfully violate the law? You could be prosecuted criminally and fined up to $10,000. A second conviction may result in imprisonment. Employers who willfully or repeatedly violate the minimum wage or overtime pay requirements are subject to civil money penalties of up to $1,000 per violation. The Department of Labor can also bring suit for back pay and an equal amount in liquidated damages.

More information can be found at:

http://www.dol.gov/elaws/flsa.htm

http://www.dol.gov/esa/

http://www.opm.gov/flsa/overview.asp

Equal Pay Act

Year Enacted: 1963

Enforced by: the Equal Employment Opportunity Commission

Applies to: Employers with two or more employees

The Equal Pay Act was created to protect both women and men from gender discrimination in pay rates, although it was passed to help rectify the wage disparity experienced by female workers. In practice, this law has mostly been applied to situations where women are paid less than men for doing similar jobs.

While the law applies to any employer with two or more employees, there must be at least one woman and one man. If the agency is made up solely of men or solely of women this law does not apply.

Most people think the law says "Equal pay for equal work." In actuality, it says, "Equal pay for equal skill, equal effort, and equal responsibility." Equal skill would include experience, training, ability, and education measured by the performance requirements of the job while equal effort is a measurement of the physical or mental exertion required to perform the job. Finally, equal responsibility is dealing with the degree of accountability required in performance of the job.

Jobs don't have to be identical for the courts to consider them equal. Titles and job descriptions are irrelevant if two employees are actually doing the same work. What matters are the duties they actually perform. Assuming everything else is the same, can you pay a man more than a woman if:

He has his CPCU and CIC designations and she doesn't?

He has been in insurance 20 years and she only has 10 years experience, even through she has been with the agency longer?

The answer in both situations is yes, because they deal with experience, training and education measured by the requirements of the job. Be careful. If a skill is not required to perform the job, you can't use it to pay one individual more than another.

Two CSRs (one male, one female) each handle the same amount of business and are identical in all other respects except that one is responsible for training new CSRs and performing desk audits of the other CSRs. Since the responsibilities are not equal, you don't have to pay them the same.

Let's assume you have two producers, one male and one female. The female has been with you for ten years and you pay her 50% on new business and 30% on renewals. The male has been with your agency five years and is paid 35% on new and 25% on renewals. You don't have a problem because of seniority. However, if you hire another female producer, everything else being the same, and you pay her 50% on new business and 30% on renewal, you have a problem. You haven't applied seniority consistently across the board.

But wait a minute, isn't it ok to pay a woman more than a man? No, the Equal Pay Act say that you can't pay employees of one sex less than employees of the opposite sex. It doesn't say anything about male or female.

OK, your agency has a problem in that (again, everything else being equal) male employees are paid more than female employees. Can you reduce the pay of the men to avoid EPA problems? No. Any wage differential based on sex has to be eliminated by raising the pay of lower paid employees, not by reducing the pay of the higher paid employees.

The best way to protect your agency from an Equal Pay Act violation is to have job descriptions that address the skill, effort, and responsibilities of every position in your agency. These job descriptions should also include compensation ranges. Spell out exactly how, why, and when the ranges could be changed, but leave them flexible enough to be able to attract the best candidates you can get without violating the Equal Pay Act.

For larger agencies you should also regularly audit your compensation system to find and correct any disparities in pay. When it comes to the Equal Pay Act, remember, be fair and be consistent.

More information can be found at:

http://www.eeoc.gov/policy/epa.html

http://www.eeoc.gov/epa/

Title VII of the Civil Rights Acts

Year enacted: 1964

Enforced by: Equal Employment Opportunity Commission (EEOC)

Applies to: Employers who have had 15 or more employees for each working day in each of 20 or more calendar weeks in the current or preceding calendar year.

Title VII is a provision of the Civil Rights Act of 1964 that prohibits discrimination in almost every employment circumstance on the basis of race, color, sex, religion, or national origin.

In essence, Title VII's protections are supposed to give every employee and candidate a fair shot at a job by forcing employers to consider only job-related criteria in making employment decisions.

Race, color, religion, gender, pregnancy, and national origin are considered protected classes under Title VII because of the history of unfair treatment each class has endured. As an employer you must consider Title VII in every step of the job application process:

1) When reviewing applications/resumes
2) During the interview of candidates
3) When testing job applicants

In addition to interviewing candidates, Title VII also is applicable when you are considering employees for promotions, transfers, or any other employment-related benefit or condition.

With the 1991 amendment, employees are now allowed to seek a jury trial and can collect compensatory and punitive damages in addition to back pay, job reinstatement, and retroactive seniority.

For more information:

http://www.eeoc.gov/policy/vii.html

Age Discrimination In Employment Act

Year enacted: 1967 (Amended in 1985)

Enforced by: Equal Employment Opportunity Commission (EEOC)

Applies to: Employers who have had 20 or more employees for each working day in each of 20 or more calendar weeks in the current or preceding calendar year.

Suppose you have an employee who is 50 years old. In which of the following situations might you have an ADEA problem if you replace the 50 year old with:

- Someone that is 32

- Someone that is 42

- Someone that is 62

Regardless as to the age of the replacement, if you terminate someone over 40 because of their age you have a problem. Can you terminate them for non-age related reasons or for cause? Absolutely. Not being able to perform the functions/duties of the position are legitimate grounds for termination. Just don't say, "Bob, you are getting older and can't perform the job up to our expectations." Say that and you lose. A better way to put it would be "Bob, based upon the job description, you are not performing the job adequately." Never, ever say they are too old to do the job.

That being said, the U.S. Supreme Court has ruled that older workers can sue over pay or benefits plans that favor younger workers, even if no evidence of <u>deliberate</u> age discrimination exists. If a workplace practice has disparate impact on employees over 40, it is discriminatory even if that practice appears neutral.

The best way for an agency to protect itself is to defend its practices based on reasonable factors other than age and by carefully reviewing the statistical consequences of its policies.

There used to be an upper age limit to the ADEA but nowadays there is no ceiling unless there is a bona fide occupational qualification (BFOQ). The best example of an age BFOQ is the requirement for airline pilots to retire at age 60. For an insurance agency, there is no valid reason for an age BFOQ.

The Older Workers Benefit Protection Act expanded the ADEA to include benefits, pensions, and early retirement incentives for employees age 40 or older.

For more information:

http://www.eeoc.gov/policy/adea.html

http://www.eeoc.gov/facts/age.html

Federal Wiretapping Act

Year enacted: 1968

Enforced by: Federal Communications Commission (FCC)

Applies to: Employers who engage in interstate commerce

Ever call a telephone company or airline reservation desk? Usually, the voicemail says something like "Your call may be recorded for quality control purposes." Is it really for quality control? Maybe. Is it a way around the Federal Wiretapping Act? Absolutely.

The FWA applies to any employers involved in interstate commerce and prohibits them from intentionally intercepting any wire, oral, or electronic communication that takes place on the premises of any business.

In 1986, the Federal Wiretap Act was amended with the Electronic Communications Privacy Act. It prohibits the intentional interception, use or disclosure of any electronic (including email), wire or oral communication. It also prohibits the unauthorized access to and disclosure of any stored wire and electronic communication. The ECPA has three exceptions, allowing employers to:

- Monitor business-related phone calls;
- Monitor communications with employee consent; and
- Retrieve and access stored email messages.

While the federal ECPA gives employers the right to monitor all e-mail traffic and Internet activity on the company system, it does not always prevent outraged employees from filing invasion-of-privacy claims.

The best way to protect your agency is to give employees explicit notice that:
- Employees do not have a reasonable expectation of privacy;
- The company has the right to monitor anything transmitted or stored on its computer system; and
- Management intends to exercise that right.

You should explain why monitoring is a business necessity and have the employees sign a memo consenting to the monitoring. Another way to notify the employees would be to put this in the Employee Handbook. Of course, make sure the employee signs a form stating that they agree to abide by the Employee Handbook.

For more information:

http://www.monnat.com/Publications/Wiretap.pdf

Fair Credit Reporting Act

Year enacted: 1970

Enforced by: Federal Trade Commission (FTC)

Applies to: Employers who engage in interstate commerce

You are interviewing candidates for a receptionist position at your agency. Can you legally pull a credit report on her? What if you are hiring a bookkeeper? The Fair Credit Reporting Act prohibits you as an employer from using credit information against employees or applicants unless you have a valid business reason.

Does your receptionist accept cash payments? The bookkeeper will undoubtedly have access to agency funds. Your CSRs and Producers will be receiving funds from clients. Even your file clerk who handles the mail may have access to money. In essence, practically everyone in the agency could have access to agency, carrier, or client funds. If an applicant has bad credit, you could have a legitimate concern about embezzlement. There is your legitimate business need.

You don't have to pull credit reports for all positions within the agency, but once you pull a report on one person, you should pull reports on all people you are actively considering for that position.

But before you pull that credit report, you must notify the applicant that you are pulling his report and obtain a written acknowledgement of the notification. (See sample on Page INSERT PAGE NUMBER) You must also give the applicant the name and phone number of the reporting agency and a statement of his rights under the law to dispute the accuracy of the report.

If you pull the credit report and it's bad, you then need to decide whether or not to hire the candidate. Before you deny employment, you must notify the applicant and give him/her the opportunity to correct any errors that may be in the report. Don't think credit-reporting companies make mistakes? Order a credit report on yourself and see how accurate it is.

The three major credit-reporting companies are TransUnion, Equifax, and Experian. Their websites are: www.transunion.com, www.equifax.com, www.experian.com

For more information:

http://www.ftc.gov/os/statutes/fcra.htm

Pregnancy Discrimination Act

Year enacted: 1978

Enforced by: Equal Employment Opportunity Commission (EEOC)

Applies to: Employers who have had 15 or more employees for each working day in each of 20 or more calendar weeks in the current or preceding calendar year.

As an employer, under the Pregnancy Discrimination Act, you are prevented from refusing to hire a pregnant woman as long as she is able to perform the major functions of her job. While you cannot create special procedures to determine an employee's ability to work, you can use any procedure used to screen other employees' ability to work.

For example, if you require employees to submit a doctor's statement concerning their inability to work before granting leave or paying sick benefits, you can require employees affected by pregnancy related conditions to submit such statements.

If you have an employee who is temporarily unable to perform her job due to pregnancy, you must treat her the same as any other temporarily disabled employee. This could include: a modified workload, disability leave, or leave without pay.

As long as the employee can perform her job, you cannot prevent her from working. If an employee has been absent from work as a result of a pregnancy related condition and recovers, you cannot require her to remain on leave until the baby's birth. Management also cannot pre-establish a beginning date for maternity leave or the length of time for maternity leave. If she wants to come back to work two days after giving birth, that is her decision. You can, however, require a doctor's note stating that she is fit to return to work. You also cannot force the employee to resign or take a leave of absence.

Basically, an agency must provide pregnant employees with the same benefits as individuals with any other short-term disability. If you pay 50% of pay for eight weeks for a short-term disability, you must do the same thing for pregnant employees. If an employer provides any benefits to workers on leave, the employer must provide the same benefits for those on leave for pregnancy related conditions. This also means that you must hold open a job for a pregnancy related absence the same length of time you would hold that job open for employees on sick or disability leave.

The PDA is an amendment to Title VII of the Civil Rights Act.

For more information:

http://www.eeoc.gov/facts/fs-preg.html

Jury Systems Improvement Act

Year enacted: 1978

Enforced by: Federal Courts

Applies to: All employers

So you have a small, four-person agency, and your CSR has just been picked as a juror for a high-profile celebrity murder case that is going to last a year. Can you fire her? Nope! The JSIA apples to all employees, regardless of the number of employees, and is enforced by the Federal Courts. You can't discharge, threaten to discharge, intimidate or coerce any employee because of their service or potential service on a jury.

And you cannot tell the employee to ask to be excused for financial hardship. That is their decision, not the decision of the employer. But do you have to pay the employee while on jury duty? No. The law doesn't say anything about paying them. While you can restrict the number of <u>paid</u> jury-duty-leave days, you cannot restrict the number of <u>unpaid</u> jury–duty-leave days.

Consolidated Budget Omnibus Reconciliation Act (COBRA)

Year enacted: 1985

Enforced by: Internal Revenue Service

Applies to: Employers with 20 or more employees on more than 50 percent of its typical business days in the previous calendar year.

COBRA allows certain terminated employees, retirees, spouses, and dependent children to temporarily continue their participation in group health insurance plans at group rates. When a qualified individual elects COBRA coverage, he/she is responsible for paying his/her full premium; the agency is not required to contribute. Additionally, the agency can charge 2% of the premium as an administrative fee.

The former employee can remain on COBRA for up to 18 months. If he becomes disabled within the first 60 days of COBRA coverage, his coverage can be extended an additional 11 months, for a total of 29 months. The employee's spouse and children can extend their coverage under certain conditions up to a maximum of 36 months.

In the event of an employee's gross misconduct, the agency does not have to offer COBRA to the terminated employee. However, what is "gross misconduct?" Like many legal terms, this one is not clearly defined. In fact, many attorneys will suggest you allow an employee terminated for gross misconduct to elect COBRA coverage since the employee is paying the full amount of the premium.

Employers must notify the employee (or plan administrator) of a qualifying event within 30 days after an employee's death, termination, reduction in hours of employment, or entitlement to Medicare. Qualified beneficiaries then have 60 days to elect coverage. This period is measured from the later of the coverage loss date or the date the COBRA election notice is provided by the employer or plan administrator.

COBRA must be offered by employers with 20 or more employees on more than 50 percent of its typical business days in the previous calendar year. Both full and part-time employees are counted to determine whether a plan is subject to COBRA. Each part-time employee counts as a fraction of an employee, with the fraction equal to the number of hours that the part-time employee worked divided by the hours an employee must work to be considered full time.

For more information:

http://www.dol.gov/dol/topic/health-plans/cobra.htm

http://www.dol.gov/ebsa/faqs/faq_consumer_cobra.html

Immigration Reform & Control Act (IRCA)

Year enacted: 1986

Enforced by: Department of Justice, Immigration and Naturalization Service

Applies to: All employers

This law requires all employers to verify the identity of prospective employees, as well as their eligibility to work in the United States. As an employer, you must complete and retain Form I-9 for three years from date of hire or one year from date of termination, whichever is longer.

There are fines ranging from $250 to $10,000 for each unauthorized alien and a maximum six-month prison sentence if the employer demonstrates a persistent pattern of hiring unauthorized aliens

For more information:

http://www.usda.gov/agency/oce/oce/labor-affairs/ircasumm.htm

Exhibit: I-9 Form

U.S. Department of Justice
Immigration and Naturalization Service

OMB No. 1115-0136

Employment Eligibility Verification

INSTRUCTIONS
PLEASE READ ALL INSTRUCTIONS CAREFULLY BEFORE COMPLETING THIS FORM.

Anti-Discrimination Notice. It is illegal to discriminate against any individual (other than an alien not authorized to work in the U.S.) in hiring, discharging, or recruiting or referring for a fee because of that individual's national origin or citizenship status. It is illegal to discriminate against work eligible individuals. Employers **CANNOT** specify which document(s) they will accept from an employee. The refusal to hire an individual because of a future expiration date may also constitute illegal discrimination.

Section 1 - Employee. All employees, citizens and noncitizens, hired after November 6, 1986, must complete Section 1 of this form at the time of hire, which is the actual beginning of employment. **The employer is responsible for ensuring that Section 1 is timely and properly completed.**

Preparer/Translator Certification. The Preparer/Translator Certification must be completed if Section 1 is prepared by a person other than the employee. A preparer/translator may be used only when the employee is unable to complete Section 1 on his/her own. However, the employee must still sign Section 1.

Section 2 - Employer. For the purpose of completing this form, the term "employer" includes those recruiters and referrers for a fee who are agricultural associations, agricultural employers or farm labor contractors.

Employers must complete Section 2 by examining evidence of identity and employment eligibility within three (3) business days of the date employment begins. If employees are authorized to work, but are unable to present the required document(s) within three business days, they must present a receipt for the application of the document(s) within three business days and the actual document(s) within ninety (90) days. However, if employers hire individuals for a duration of less than three business days, Section 2 must be completed at the time employment begins. **Employers must record: 1)** document title; **2)** issuing authority; **3)** document number, **4)** expiration date, if any; and **5)** the date employment begins. Employers must sign and date the certification. Employees must present original documents. Employers may, but are not required to, photocopy the document(s) presented. These photocopies may only be used for the verification process and must be retained with the I-9. **However, employers are still responsible for completing the I-9.**

Section 3 - Updating and Reverification. Employers must complete Section 3 when updating and/or reverifying the I-9. Employers must reverify employment eligibility of their employees on or before the expiration date recorded in Section 1. Employers **CANNOT** specify which document(s) they will accept from an employee.

- If an employee's name has changed at the time this form is being updated/ reverified, complete Block A.

- If an employee is rehired within three (3) years of the date this form was originally completed and the employee is still eligible to be employed on the same basis as previously indicated on this form (updating), complete Block B and the signature block.

- If an employee is rehired within three (3) years of the date this form was originally completed and the employee's work authorization has expired **or** if a current employee's work authorization is about to expire (reverification), complete Block B and:
  - examine any document that reflects that the employee is authorized to work in the U.S. (see List A **or** C),
  - record the document title, document number and expiration date (if any) in Block C, and complete the signature block.

Photocopying and Retaining Form I-9. A blank I-9 may be reproduced, provided both sides are copied. The Instructions must be available to all employees completing this form. Employers must retain completed I-9s for three (3) years after the date of hire or one (1) year after the date employment ends, whichever is later.

For more detailed information, you may refer to the INS Handbook for Employers, (Form M-274). You may obtain the handbook at your local INS office.

Privacy Act Notice. The authority for collecting this information is the Immigration Reform and Control Act of 1986, Pub. L. 99-603 (8 USC 1324a).

This information is for employers to verify the eligibility of individuals for employment to preclude the unlawful hiring, or recruiting or referring for a fee, of aliens who are not authorized to work in the United States.

This information will be used by employers as a record of their basis for determining eligibility of an employee to work in the United States. The form will be kept by the employer and made available for inspection by officials of the U.S. Immigration and Naturalization Service, the Department of Labor and the Office of Special Counsel for Immigration Related Unfair Employment Practices.

Submission of the information required in this form is voluntary. However, an individual may not begin employment unless this form is completed, since employers are subject to civil or criminal penalties if they do not comply with the Immigration Reform and Control Act of 1986.

Reporting Burden. We try to create forms and instructions that are accurate, can be easily understood and which impose the least possible burden on you to provide us with information. Often this is difficult because some immigration laws are very complex. Accordingly, the reporting burden for this collection of information is computed as follows: **1)** learning about this form, 5 minutes; **2)** completing the form, 5 minutes; and **3)** assembling and filing (recordkeeping) the form, 5 minutes, for an average of 15 minutes per response. If you have comments regarding the accuracy of this burden estimate, or suggestions for making this form simpler, you can write to the Immigration and Naturalization Service, HQPDI, 425 I Street, N.W., Room 4034, Washington, DC 20536. OMB No. 1115-0136.

EMPLOYERS MUST RETAIN COMPLETED FORM I-9
PLEASE DO NOT MAIL COMPLETED FORM I-9 TO INS

Form I-9 (Rev. 11-21-91)N

U.S. Department of Justice
Immigration and Naturalization Service

OMB No. 1115-0136

Employment Eligibility Verification

Please read instructions carefully before completing this form. The instructions must be available during completion of this form. ANTI-DISCRIMINATION NOTICE: It is illegal to discriminate against work eligible individuals. Employers CANNOT specify which document(s) they will accept from an employee. The refusal to hire an individual because of a future expiration date may also constitute illegal discrimination.

Section 1. Employee Information and Verification. To be completed and signed by employee at the time employment begins.

Print Name: Last	First	Middle Initial	Maiden Name

Address (Street Name and Number) | Apt. # | Date of Birth (month/day/year)

City | State | Zip Code | Social Security #

I am aware that federal law provides for imprisonment and/or fines for false statements or use of false documents in connection with the completion of this form.

I attest, under penalty of perjury, that I am (check one of the following):
☐ A citizen or national of the United States
☐ A Lawful Permanent Resident (Alien # A_____
☐ An alien authorized to work until ___/___/___
(Alien # or Admission #) _____

Employee's Signature | Date (month/day/year)

Preparer and/or Translator Certification. *(To be completed and signed if Section 1 is prepared by a person other than the employee.) I attest, under penalty of perjury, that I have assisted in the completion of this form and that to the best of my knowledge the information is true and correct.*

Preparer's/Translator's Signature | Print Name

Address (Street Name and Number, City, State, Zip Code) | Date (month/day/year)

Section 2. Employer Review and Verification. To be completed and signed by employer. Examine one document from List A OR examine one document from List B and one from List C, as listed on the reverse of this form, and record the title, number and expiration date, if any, of the document(s)

List A	OR	**List B**	AND	**List C**
Document title:_____		_____		_____
Issuing authority:_____		_____		_____
Document #:_____		_____		_____
Expiration Date (if any): ___/___/___		___/___/___		___/___/___
Document #:_____				
Expiration Date (if any): ___/___/___				

CERTIFICATION - I attest, under penalty of perjury, that I have examined the document(s) presented by the above-named employee, that the above-listed document(s) appear to be genuine and to relate to the employee named, that the employee began employment on *(month/day/year)* ___/___/___ **and that to the best of my knowledge the employee is eligible to work in the United States. (State employment agencies may omit the date the employee began employment.)**

Signature of Employer or Authorized Representative | Print Name | Title

Business or Organization Name | Address (Street Name and Number, City, State, Zip Code) | Date (month/day/year)

Section 3. Updating and Reverification. To be completed and signed by employer.

A. New Name (if applicable) | B. Date of rehire (month/day/year) (if applicable)

C. If employee's previous grant of work authorization has expired, provide the information below for the document that establishes current employment eligibility.

Document Title:_____ | Document #:_____ | Expiration Date (if any): ___/___/___

I attest, under penalty of perjury, that to the best of my knowledge, this employee is eligible to work in the United States, and if the employee presented document(s), the document(s) I have examined appear to be genuine and to relate to the individual.

Signature of Employer or Authorized Representative | Date (month/day/year)

Form I-9 (Rev. 11-21-91)N Page 2

LISTS OF ACCEPTABLE DOCUMENTS

LIST A		LIST B		LIST C
Documents that Establish Both Identity and Employment Eligibility	**OR**	**Documents that Establish Identity**	**AND**	**Documents that Establish Employment Eligibility**

LIST A — Documents that Establish Both Identity and Employment Eligibility

1. U.S. Passport (unexpired or expired)

2. Certificate of U.S. Citizenship (INS Form N-560 or N-561)

3. Certificate of Naturalization (INS Form N-550 or N-570)

4. Unexpired foreign passport, with I-551 stamp or attached INS Form I-94 indicating unexpired employment authorization

5. Permanent Resident Card or Alien Registration Receipt Card with photograph (INS Form I-151 or I-551)

6. Unexpired Temporary Resident Card (INS Form I-688)

7. Unexpired Employment Authorization Card (INS Form I-688A)

8. Unexpired Reentry Permit (INS Form I-327)

9. Unexpired Refugee Travel Document (INS Form I-571)

10. Unexpired Employment Authorization Document issued by the INS which contains a photograph (INS Form I-688B)

OR

LIST B — Documents that Establish Identity

1. Driver's license or ID card issued by a state or outlying possession of the United States provided it contains a photograph or information such as name, date of birth, gender, height, eye color and address

2. ID card issued by federal, state or local government agencies or entities, provided it contains a photograph or information such as name, date of birth, gender, height, eye color and address

3. School ID card with a photograph

4. Voter's registration card

5. U.S. Military card or draft record

6. Military dependent's ID card

7. U.S. Coast Guard Merchant Mariner Card

8. Native American tribal document

9. Driver's license issued by a Canadian government authority

For persons under age 18 who are unable to present a document listed above:

10. School record or report card

11. Clinic, doctor or hospital record

12. Day-care or nursery school record

AND

LIST C — Documents that Establish Employment Eligibility

1. U.S. social security card issued by the Social Security Administration (other than a card stating it is not valid for employment)

2. Certification of Birth Abroad issued by the Department of State (Form FS-545 or Form DS-1350)

3. Original or certified copy of a birth certificate issued by a state, county, municipal authority or outlying possession of the United States bearing an official seal

4. Native American tribal document

5. U.S. Citizen ID Card (INS Form I-197)

6. ID Card for use of Resident Citizen in the United States (INS Form I-179)

7. Unexpired employment authorization document issued by the INS (other than those listed under List A)

Illustrations of many of these documents appear in Part 8 of the Handbook for Employers (M-274)

Form I-9 (Rev. 10/4/00)Y Page 3

Employee Polygraph Protection Act

Year enacted: 1988

Enforced by: Department of Labor

Applies to: All employers with two or more employees and at least $500,000 in revenues.

The EPPA prohibits most employers from requiring or requesting pre-employment polygraphs of applicants. Some types of businesses, such as armored cars, security systems, and companies manufacturing controlled substances are allowed to give pre-employment polygraphs, but insurance agencies are not among them.

So what about testing existing employees? Let's assume money is stolen from the agency's safe. Can the agency test all its employees? No. Employers can administer tests during an ongoing investigation of financial loss or injury through theft, embezzlement, or misappropriation, assuming reasonable suspicion of the employee's guilt. The suspected employee must also have access to the property involved.

If the safe is kept locked, you can give a polygraph test only to those employees who have the combination to the safe. Since the receptionist doesn't have access, you can't test her.

More information can be found at:

http://www.fas.org/sgp/othergov/polygraph/eppa.html

http://www.dol.gov/esa/regs/statutes/whd/poly01.pdf

American with Disabilities Act

Year enacted: 1990

Enforced by: Equal Employment Opportunity Commission (EEOC)

Applies to: Employers who have had 15 or more employees for each working day in each of 20 or more calendar weeks in the current or preceding calendar year.

The Americans with Disabilities Act (ADA) is a federal anti-discrimination law whose purpose is to guarantee equal opportunities to individuals with disabilities, those with a history of disability, and those perceived to be disabled. Equal opportunity applies to the job application process, hiring and firing, advancement, compensation, job training, and other conditions of employment. But what is a disability? According to the law, a disability is a physical or mental impairment that substantially limits one or more major life activities.

This law requires employers to base hiring decisions solely on the ability of the individual to perform the essential functions of the job. In addition to employment, the ADA bans discrimination in public services, transportation, public accommodation, and telecommunications.

Employers must also provide reasonable accommodations to disabled individuals. There are two words that need to be defined here, "reasonable" and "accommodation." What is an accommodation? It's a job modification that allows an individual with a disability to perform the job's essential functions. Reasonable accommodations could include:

- Making facilities accessible and usable by disabled people
- Job restructuring
- Modifying work schedules
- Acquiring or modifying equipment
- Adjusting or modifying policies

But what is reasonable? It's an accommodation that wouldn't impose an "undue hardship" on the business. In many cases, the courts will decide whether or not an accommodation is "reasonable." What should you as an agency owner do to comply with the American with Disabilities Act?

Job Descriptions. Develop job descriptions that document the essential functions of each job.

Job Tests. Define any job-related tests applicants must pass after a conditional offer of employment has been made.

<u>Task Screenings.</u> Conduct task screenings to determine whether an individual is qualified for a specific job.

<u>Medical Screenings.</u> You cannot conduct a medical exam on an applicant before a conditional offer of employment has been made. Medical tests do NOT have to be job-related, but results from the medical screening cannot be used in the hire/no hire decision unless they are job-related. Medical tests must be required of every employee entering into the same job category, regardless of the disability.

Additional information is available at:

http://www.usdoj.gov/crt/ada/adahom1.htm

Family & Medical Leave Act

Year enacted: 1993

Enforced by: Department of Labor

Applies to: Companies with 50 or more employees within a 75-mile radius.

If an employee has been employed 12 months with the agency and with 1,250 hours of service in the preceding 12 months, the Family Medical Leave Act allows the employee to take up to 12 weeks of <u>unpaid</u> leave for:

1. The birth of a child
2. Their own serious health condition
3. To care for a family member with a serious health condition, or
4. The placement of a child for adoption or foster care.

It should be noted that the 12 weeks of unpaid leave do not have to be taken in one block of time. Intermittent leave as well as a reduced work schedule are also permissible. As a result, you may need to rearrange the job functions of other workers or hire a temporary to cover the responsibilities of the absent employee. The employee should, whenever possible, provide reasonable notice to the employer.

The FMLA requires employers to:

1. Allow eligible employees to take up to 12 weeks of unpaid leave for the above circumstances.
2. Provide continued health benefits during leave.
3. Restore employees to the same position upon return from leave (or to a position with the same pay, benefits, and terms and conditions of employment).
4. Notify employees of their rights and responsibilities under the Act.

While FMLA is for unpaid leave, employers may choose to use an employee's accrued paid vacation leave, personal leave, or sick leave for any part of the 12-week period. This would prevent the employee from taking 12 weeks FMLA leave and then taking additional time off for vacation. In the event the employer utilizes an employee's paid leave, the employer must, obviously, pay the employee for that time.

Spouses working for the same employer are limited to a total of 12 weeks combined unpaid leave. An exception to this is when one spouse is caring for the other spouse who has a serious health condition.

When an employee is ready to return from FMLA leave, as long as it has not exceeded the 12 weeks permitted, he/she must be restored to an equivalent position with equivalent pay, benefits, and terms and conditions of employment. The employer may reasonably require recertification of continued leave and/or certification of fitness to return to work. However, FMLA does not protect against workforce reductions (layoffs).

Additional information is available at:

http://www.dol.gov/esa/whd/fmla/

The following are some common law concepts that are applicable to insurance agencies.

Employment at Will

As stated earlier in this section, the employment at will concept allows the employer or employee to sever the employment relationship at any time and for any reason, either with or without cause, unless prohibited by law or an employment contract.

Exceptions to employment at will include:

- A real contract

- An implied contract - This could be a verbal or written statement implying that employment will be continued. (This is why you should say "regular employee" and never "permanent employee" in your employee handbook.

- Public Policy - An employee cannot be fired for fulfilling legal obligations or for performing actions that are considered to be socially useful. Examples of this include serving on jury duty, filing for workers compensation benefits, or reporting criminal wrongdoing.

- Implied covenant of good faith and fair dealing - Employees, especially those who are long-term, should not be dealt with arbitrarily or capriciously.

Sometimes people think that if a state is a "right to work" state that it is the opposite of employment at will. These two terms are not related. "Right to work" deals with an individual's right to work at a company that has a union, regardless of union membership.

Negligent Hiring

As the agency owner, you decide to hire someone as an outside producer. This individual is regularly out on the road making calls on clients and prospects. You never bothered to pull an MVR on him. Do you have a problem? Possibly.

Let's assume this new employee has been previously convicted of drunk driving. Your new agent takes a CSR to visit a client, but unbeknownst to the CSR, the agent has been drinking. He gets into an accident and the CSR is hurt. A breathalyzer test is given showing your agent is drunk. The CSR may have a claim against you under the concept of negligent hiring.

Employers have a duty to protect workers, customers, and visitors from injury caused by employees whom the owner knew, or should have known, posed a risk. You should not hire or retain employees who engage in wrongful acts either during or after working hours.

Defamation

Defamation is injuring someone's reputation. It can be either spoken (slander) or written (libel). So you get a telephone call from another agency about a former employee whom you terminated for misconduct. Should you say anything or should you keep your mouth shut?

Most agency owners keep their mouths shut for fear of a defamation lawsuit. But it's not that easy to prove defamation. The employee must show not only that the false report caused harm, but also that the employer made the statement with malice. The key point here is that you, as the employer, issued a false report. If you tell the truth, there is no defamation.

A conditional privilege is to be considered when you are providing complete and accurate references to a new employer about a former employee. It is necessary to help that new employer avoid potential negligent hire lawsuits. Be cautious, as even giving a good reference can harm you if you lie.

Invasion of Privacy

You look in an employee's desk and find something that tells you that he/she is having an affair with a client, a competitor, or another employee. Do you have a problem with invasion of privacy? Maybe. What is the business purpose for looking in that desk?

If you are doing a desk audit or looking for an endorsement, you have a good reason. If you are just being nosey, you are invading his/her privacy. Any unnecessary intrusion into an employee's personal life (which occurred when you looked inside that desk) may be considered an invasion of privacy.

The easiest way around this issue is to state in the employee handbook that the desk is company property and that management reserves the right to look inside it anytime management wants. By doing this, you have put the employee on notice not to leave anything in her desk she doesn't want others to know about.

Constructive Discharge

You take away the agent's laptop, you continue to provide other agents with leads, but not him/her, and you discontinue the expense account. If the producer quits, you could have a problem.

Constructive discharge is when the employer makes conditions so intolerable for an employee that the employee must resign. Legally this is considered an involuntary termination, not a resignation. At the very least, the employee has a case to collect unemployment. If you want to fire someone, fire the producer. Don't force him/her to quit.

Section 3: Job Descriptions

The Need for Job Descriptions

As stated previously, 60 to 70 percent of every dollar of agency revenue goes out in compensation expense. For an agency to be successful and profitable, it needs to properly manage its human resources.

But before you begin to hire people, you need to know exactly what you want them to do, and you need to share that with them during the interview process. The worst thing a candidate can hear is, "You have a great opportunity; you can create your own job description."

There are several things wrong with this:

1) What if the employee-developed job description is not what the agency needs?

2) What if the job description doesn't tie in to the agency workflow, procedures, or organization?

3) What if the there are missing functions in the job description?

4) What if the standards (if any) outlined by the employee are not acceptable to the agency?

5) What if you have more than one person in that position?

Depending on the stage of organizational growth, the agency will need to determine the organizational structure, the number and types of employees it needs. Based on these factors, the agency must decide what functions go with which job, and then create job descriptions.

A job description should establish the basic performance requirements of the position, as well as set the needed qualities and qualifications for potential candidates seeking the position. Whenever possible, it should clarify acceptable performance and describe in detail the position's activities.

Comparing job descriptions for different positions in the agency should help the agency establish the "worth" of the position and aid in setting levels of compensation. Obviously, this needs to be done prior to hiring someone.

Additionally, job descriptions can help in determining whether an employee is exempt under the Fair Law Standards Act and whether a disabled candidate can meet the job requirements (see American with Disabilities Act).

Once the agency has completed the job descriptions, they also become useful hiring tools, as interviewers share them with candidates and ask related questions, such as:

1) What functions of the job description have you done for previous employers?

2) Which of these functions do you do extremely well? Give some examples.

3) Are you weak in any of these areas?

4) Which of these functions do you like to perform?

5) Which functions do you dislike performing?

6) Is there anything preventing you from adequately performing all the functions on the job description?

After the employee has been hired, the job description should be an integral part of the performance evaluation.

Many agencies don't have job descriptions because they think this process is an overwhelming task and they don't have the time. Those problems can be overcome by starting with samples (see pages 80-112) and having the employees currently holding those positions edit the descriptions to fit your agency, then merging the results with manager input to create a standardized job description for each job.

What should be in a job description? While there are many formats, most include the following:

1) Title, Reporting Hierarchy and Compensation

2) Summary

3) Position Functions

4) Knowledge, Skills and Abilities

5) Other Requirements

6) Working Conditions

7) General / Other

8) Acknowledgement by Employee

You should include the position title and the manager or supervisor to whom that position reports to as well as the compensation range. Some agencies prefer to not include compensation because they don't want employees who earn below the maxmum asking for a raise to the maximum. If this is the case in your agency, set a compensation range for each position that is available only to management. Distribute the completed job descriptions to all employees on a position-by-position basis.

A brief one- or two-paragraph summary of the position should identify why the employer has hired the person and what the position accomplishes in the overall performance of the agency.

The Position Functions should outline the specific nature, duties, and essential functions of the job. Whenever possible, you should make the functions as quantitative as possible. For example, let's say the receptionist's job description says, "Answers the telephone." If she answers it in 17 rings, she has accomplished the task. A better description would be "Answers the telephone within three rings in a professional and courteous manner." That can be measured.

Make sure that somewhere in the Position Functions section it states "Performs other functions as assigned by management." The one thing you do not want to hear from an employee is "It's not my job." This trumps the employee's ability to say that.

The Knowledge, Skills, and Abilities section should address the type of person you are looking for in terms of personality type and communication skills. The Other Requirements section should address licensing, automation, and software skills, etc.
Working Conditions refers to the type of office you have. Is it quiet and slow or a fast-paced environment? Do employees have the luxury of working on one duty at a time or is multi-tasking necessary?

Use the General Section primarily for disclaimers: that other job functions may arise, that the job description is not a contract, and that it is subject to change at management's sole discretion.

Once you have finalized the job descriptions, it is important to have each employee acknowledge and sign off on the job description.

On the following pages are job descriptions for:

- **Customer Service Representative** – This can be edited so that you end up with one job description for personal lines and a somewhat different job description for commercial lines.

- **Administrative Assistant** – Some agencies may incorporate these functions into the Office Manager or Receptionist positions.

- **Automation Manager** – Deals with the agency's automation system. It is possible that someone in your agency could wear two hats (e.g. the Accountant is also responsible for automation duties). If this is the case, you can either have one person sign two different job descriptions, or the job descriptions can be tailored to your situation.

- **Accountant** – Handles all the internal accounting functions. If an outside individual does some functions, such as tax returns, you would need to delete those functions.

- **Claims Manager** – Some agencies have a person handling claims; others let the carriers handle all the claims functions; or you may prefer to transfer some of these functions to the CSR position.

- **Department Manager** – As with the CSR position, you may want to edit this position so that you end up with one job description for a Personal Lines Department Manager and another for a Commercial Lines Department Manager.

- **Mail/File Clerk** – If your agency is large enough, you might want to separate the mail and filing functions. If your agency is small, you may consider adding these functions to other job descriptions.

- **Marketing Manager** – In many agencies, this position is responsible for determining which accounts are placed with which carriers as well as carrier relationships.

- **Office Manager** – This person is responsible for the day-to-day non-insurance-related policies and procedures of the agency.

- **President** – These functions might be divided among different individuals if your agency has more than one owner.

- **Sales Manager** – If your agency is large enough, you may have one position that is responsible for managing the Producers as well as controlling the agency's sales functions.

- **CSR Assistant** – Again, if your agency is large enough, this is omeone who will assist the Customer Service Representatives with clerical functions and possibly data entry functions.

- **Producer** – Here you will want to outline what responsibilities the producers have when it comes to writing new business and being involved in renewals.

- **Receptionist** – In most agencies, this position serves as the initial point of contact for all office visitors and incoming telephone calls.

- **Telemarketer** – If your agency is large enough, this position is responsible for lead generation and setting appointments for producers.

If you don't already have job descriptions, the next step is to tailor these job descriptions to your agency. Distribute the descriptions to the person currently holding that position, and ask him/her to:

1) Review the description for accuracy.

2) Add any functions the employee is doing that are not on the description.

3) Delete any functions the employee is not doing.

4) Adjust quantitative aspects of descriptions to fit what is appropriate for your agency.

Once this is done, the job descriptions should be collected and reviewed by managers or supervisors as well as human resources personnel. Determine if any deleted function would be more appropriate for someone else in your agency. Also make sure that the descriptions tie into your workflow or procedures manual.

Exhibit: Customer Service Representative Job Description

Customer Service Representative Job Description

Position Title: Customer Service Representative

Reports to: _____

Compensation Range: _____ to _____

A. SUMMARY

Assists in the production of new accounts and the retention of existing accounts. Provides prompt, efficient, high-quality service to designated accounts in support of Producer activities.

B. POSITION FUNCTIONS

1. Responsible for gathering the information and risk management recommendations for the renewal of designated accounts sixty days prior to renewal and for delivering renewals and/or binders for designated accounts, as needed, within five days of receipt.

2. Conducts periodic service calls for designated accounts.

3. Performs special projects at the request of designated clients after being approved by manager. Binders and/or policy or endorsement requests are to be completed within three days of date quoted to client.

4. Maintains a concern for timeliness and completeness when interacting with customers, agency and company personnel to minimize potential for errors & omissions claims.

5. After reviewing updated client exposure survey information, obtains other renewal information from insured, and completes applications for designated renewal business sixty days before renewal date. Assists Producer(s) as needed.

6. Reviews renewals to determine if non-standard policies can be rewritten in a standard program. Prepares rewrite applications for business through companies no longer represented at least 30 days prior to renewal. Secures and submits required renewal underwriting information.

7. Receives phone calls and office visitors requesting quotes, changes to existing coverage and/or new policies. Completes changes/requests within 24 hours of receipt. Determines acceptability and placement, completes applications or endorsements, and collects premium when applicable.

8. Reviews existing accounts to determine if additional lines of insurance should be solicited and does so by mail and/or phone prior to renewal.

9. Receives and reviews all terminations and cancellations to determine action to be taken, and takes needed action within 72 hours of receipt.

10. Handles premium collection through form letters and requests cancellation of policies when necessary.

Page 1 of 2

11. Follows up on outstanding claims and provides assistance in their resolution, as necessary.

12. Solicits expiration dates for policies not written by agency. Expectations are an average of one expiration date per client serviced.

13. Actively solicits increases in limits and/or coverages or rounding out accounts through sales to clients at every service contact.

14. Actively seeks referrals from current client base to solicit for new business prospects; follows up to generate new business using prospect database and automation system. Expectation is five referrals per week.

15. Documents all material conversations with insureds and/or carriers regarding exposures and coverages.

16. Performs other functions as assigned by management.

C. KNOWLEDGE, SKILLS AND ABILITIES

Must be an assertive self-starter with the ability to influence others. Should have demonstrated effective presentation skills through both verbal and written communications. Must be willing to travel as required.

D. OTHER REQUIREMENTS

Must have all licenses as required by the State Department of Insurance to discuss and/or sell insurance in states where the agency functions. Ability to use personal computer, calculator, agency automation system, and proficiency in various software programs, including but not limited to Microsoft Word and Excel.

E. WORKING CONDITIONS

Fast-paced multi-tasking environment.

F. GENERAL

1. This job description is intended to describe the level of work required of the person performing the job.

2. Essential functions are outlined; other duties may be assigned as needs arise or as required to support the agency's essential functions.

3. This description is not intended as a contract and is subject to unilateral change and revision by management.

4. Any written contractual agreements will supersede this job description.

5. All requirements may be modified to reasonably accommodate physically or mentally challenged employees.

I have read, understand, and agree to abide by the job description.

_____   _____
Signature   Date

Exhibit: Administrative Assistant Job Description

Administrative Assistant Job Description

Position Title: Administrative Assistant

Reports to: _____

Compensation Range: _____ to _____

A. SUMMARY

Provides assistance and administrative support for all areas of the agency.

B. POSITION FUNCTIONS

1. Processes typed material on word processing equipment.

2. Purchases and inventories agency supplies.

3. Organizes all executive meetings and conferences.

4. Monitors expenses for telephone and postage so that any cost savings can be recognized and implemented.

5. Programs and communicates to affected employees all new material for form letters within 48 hours of receipt.

6. Types dictated material and proofreads all typewritten material to ensure error-free content.

7. Distributes all typewritten material as per instructions of requester.

8. Performs other functions as assigned by management.

C. KNOWLEDGE, SKILLS AND ABILITIES

Must be organized, with demonstrated skills for effective verbal and written communication. Should be familiar with business operations at the corporate level and should have a good understanding of the agency system. Must be highly knowledgeable about the mechanics and applications of word processing programs.

D. OTHER REQUIREMENTS

Ability to use personal computer, calculator, agency automation system, and proficiency in various software programs, including but not limited to Microsoft Word and Excel.

E. WORKING CONDITIONS

Fast-paced multi-tasking environment.

Page 1 of 2

F. GENERAL

1. This job description is intended to describe the level of work required of the person performing the job.

2. Essential functions are outlined; other duties may be assigned as needs arise or as required to support the agency's essential functions.

3. This description is not intended as a contract and is subject to unilateral change and revision by management.

4. Any written contractual agreements will supersede this job description.

5. All requirements may be modified to reasonably accommodate physically or mentally challenged employees.

I have read, understand, and agree to abide by the job description.

_____   _____

Signature   Date

Page 2 of 2

Exhibit: Automation Manager Job Description

Automation Manager Job Description

Position Title: Automation Manager

Reports to: _____

Compensation Range: _____ to _____

A. SUMMARY

Accurately and efficiently maintains the agency's automated information system. Trains staff on system usage, resolves problems, performs accuracy audits, maintains historical logs and system backup files, and accesses and utilizes the system's tracking and reporting capabilities. Responsible for making cost-effective recommendations on appropriate updates and revisions to hardware and software to ensure agency efficiency. Develops reports and programs related to the system for supervisors, managers, and other users who have specific needs. Provides accurate statistics for managers and supervisors to utilize in managing their departments.

B. POSITION FUNCTIONS

1. Understands and maintains the agency's hardware and software, keeping user downtime to a minimum. Performs a majority of single-user's function and duties during hours when most employees do not use the system.

2. Provides continuous support and training of office staff related to in-house automation systems.

3. Develops and maintains procedures manual for computer and associated systems.

4. Maintains all electronic equipment including telephones, printers, mailing machines, and all computer equipment.

5. Develops and coordinates use of automated systems among departments.

6. Provides reports as required by management to monitor performance of profit centers. Reports are distributed within 24 hours of request.

7. Maintains and develops internal procedures for maintaining soft and/or hard copy files in accordance with state requirements.

8. Maintains expiration system.

9. Maintains diary system for sales and underwriting departments.

10. Works with Sales Manager and Producers in implementing and further developing marketing and prospecting system.

Page 1 of 3

11. Negotiates with equipment vendors.

12. Determines ongoing equipment and software requirements and makes recommendations to management.

13. Works directly with system vendors to quickly solve problems as they occur.

14. Determines each employee's equipment requirements and fulfills the requirements within time and cost limits established by management.

15. Maintains an awareness of new or improved hardware and software products that could affect and enhance the agency operation.

16. Customizes the agency management system when necessary to best conform to agency information needs.

17. Regularly holds or attends meetings of the system user group.

18. Implements third-party software where appropriate.

19. Maintains historical logs, runs regular system backup, and enters updates immediately upon receipt.

20. Performs other functions as assigned by management.

C. KNOWLEDGE, SKILLS AND ABILITIES

Ability to predict and evaluate the results of changes to the agency's automation system. Working knowledge of current automation research and development that could affect the agency. Ability to listen to requests from agency automation system users and translate the request into a system which best fits agency needs. Excellent understanding of agency workflow and procedures. Ability and flexibility to understand new system capabilities and appropriate applications. Expertise in using personal computer, calculator, agency automation systems, and various software, including but not limited to Microsoft Word and Excel.

D. OTHER REQUIREMENTS

Education: Four-year college degree with emphasis on information systems and management, or equivalent working experience.

E. WORKING CONDITIONS

Fast-paced, multi-tasking environment.

F. GENERAL

1. This job description is intended to describe the level of work required of the person performing the job.

2. Essential functions are outlined; other duties may be assigned as needs arise or as required to support the agency's essential functions.

3. This description is not intended as a contract and is subject to unilateral change and revision by management.

4. Any written contractual agreements will supersede this job description.

5. All requirements may be modified to reasonably accommodate physically or mentally challenged employees.

I have read, understand, and agree to abide by the job description.

_____   _____

Signature   Date

Exhibit: Accountant Job Description

Accountant Job Description

Position Title: Accountant

Reports To: _____

Compensation Range: _____ to _____

A. SUMMARY

Responsible for accurately maintaining all of the financial records of the agency. Oversees all administrative, non-insurance related functions of the agency. Administers all activities relating to Human Resource management.

B. ESSENTIAL FUNCTIONS

1. Implements and maintains security procedures for the agency's financial records, cash on hand, and all equipment.

2. Manages the agency's established credit and collection policies and procedures. Keeps bad debts to less than 1% of agency-billed commissions.

3. Ensures that all accounting systems, procedures, and insurance company regulations are communicated to and complied with by all agency personnel.

4. Establishes, prepares and maintains financial reports. Distributes reports within three days after end of month.

5. Manages and monitors expenses and cash flow.

6. Manages cash on hand and maximizes investment opportunities.

7. Handles all tax reporting requirements so that no tax payment will incur a late penalty.

8. Manages, develops and monitors the agency budget.

9. Implements all compliance reporting to outside agencies.

10. Negotiates and maintains all non-insurance-related contracts for the agency.

11. Maintains and audits special accounts: (e.g. petty cash, workers compensation, depreciation, and agency and direct bill transactions).

12. Prepares journal entries on customer accounts when requested by authorized parties.

13. Assists CSRs with invoicing problems.

Page 1 of 2

14. Acts as backup to Automation Manager when he/she is unavailable.

15. Performs other functions as assigned by management.

C. KNOWLEDGE, SKILLS AND ABILITIES

Possesses excellent verbal and written communication and organizational skills. Has familiarity with all insurance agency accounting operations. Demonstrates math skills, including the ability to add, subtract, multiply, and divide whole numbers and do calculations involving decimals and simple fractions. Is able to copy data accurately from one source to another.

D. OTHER REQUIREMENTS

Thorough understanding of generally accepted accounting practices (GAAP), financial reporting practices, budgeting, and corporate planning. Tax experience and automation skills preferred. College degree and professional designation or equivalent with minimum five years of management experience in the field of accounting, preferably with insurance operations. Ability to use personal computer, calculator, agency automation system and various software including but not limited to Microsoft Word and Excel.

E. WORKING CONDITIONS

Fast-paced multi-tasking environment.

F. GENERAL

1. This job description is intended to describe the level of work required of the person performing the job.

2. Essential functions are outlined; other duties may be assigned as needs arise or as required to support the agency's essential functions.

3. This description is not intended as a contract and is subject to unilateral change and revision by management.

4. Any written contractual agreements will supersede this job description.

5. All requirements may be modified to reasonably accommodate physically or mentally challenged employees.

I have read, understand, and agree to abide by the job description.

_____   _____

Signature   Date

Exhibit: Claims Manager Job Description

Claims Manager Job Description

Position Title: Claims Manager

Reports to: _____

Compensation Range: _____ to _____

A. SUMMARY

Provides prompt, effective assistance to clients and third parties reporting and settling claims with our agency. Also acts as a liaison between the agency and carriers and assists others in the agency with service regarding claims activity.

B. POSITION FUNCTIONS

1. Reports loss information to the appropriate insurance company the same day it is received.

2. Gives prompt and courteous service on a same-day basis to all clients. Advises insureds and claimants what processes are necessary for loss settlement.

3. Follows up with insurance companies for the timely and accurate settlement of losses.

4. Responds to customers' inquiries and questions regarding the status of a loss within 24 hours of inquiry.

5. Follows all systems, procedures, and insurance company regulations.

6. Authorizes claim payments within agency authority.

7. Prepares regular claim reports for management, as required.

8. Follows up with carriers for reserves and/or closing amounts on a regular basis.

9. Notifies producer and/or management of severe losses or reserves over $20,000. Provides ouarterly updates to management and/or appropriate CSR and Producer for clients with severe and or frequent losses.

10. Oversees maintenance of loss history including recording of payments and closure of claims.

11. Coordinates, as necessary, any activities between clients and claims adjusters.

12. Maintains knowledge of claims reporting processes and develops relationship with claims managers and supervisors for all carriers represented.

13. Notifies CSRs and/or Producers of destruction or loss of an insured risk.

14. Immediately forwards summons, suits, and other notices of legal actions to proper personnel at company level.

Page 1 of 2

15. Extends full courtesy and assistance to third parties reporting claims or providing claims information.

16. Deals promptly and with full integrity with all carrier claims personnel, responding within 24 hours to any request for action or information.

17. Prepares workers' comp and automobile claim kits or claim forms when required or as requested.

18. Visits carriers to promote goodwill and to learn their procedures so as to better advise our clients who have claims.

19. Documents all material conversations with insureds and/or carriers regarding exposures and coverages.

20. Performs other functions as assigned by management.

C. KNOWLEDGE, SKILLS AND ABILITIES

Self-starter with good verbal and written communication skills. Thorough understanding of all insurance coverages and claims procedures. Ability to use personal computer, calculator, agency automation systems, and various software programs, including but not limited to Microsoft Word and Excel.

D. OTHER REQUIREMENTS

College education or equivalent insurance experience. All licenses to discuss or place insurance as required by the State Department of Insurance in states where the agency functions.

E. WORKING CONDITIONS

Fast-paced multi-tasking environment.

F. GENERAL

1. This job description is intended to describe the level of work required of the person performing the job.

2. Essential functions are outlined; other duties may be assigned as needs arise or as required to support the agency's essential functions.

3. This description is not intended as a contract and is subject to unilateral change and revision by management.

4. Any written contractual agreements will supersede this job description.

5. All requirements may be modified to reasonably accommodate physically or mentally challenged employees.

I have read, understand, and agree to abide by the job description.

_____   _____

Signature   Date

Exhibit: Department Manager Job Description

Department Manager Job Description

Position Title: Department Manager
Reports To: _____
Compensation Range: _____ to _____

A. SUMMARY

Manages _____ Department employees to assure customer satisfaction. Is responsible for the planning, organizing, staffing, and operational activities of the department.

B. POSITION FUNCTIONS

1. Participates in the evaluation of carrier relationships.

2. Provides programs for training employees in department.

3. Performs regular reviews of subordinates, provides staff with feedback on performance issues, and sets individual goals with department employees.

4. Is able to perform all the job functions of those supervised and is able to provide backup when necessary.

5. Develops and implements customer satisfaction monitoring processes.

6. Conducts performance management activities for the department.

7. Oversees the development and implementation of new or improved department procedures.

8. Develops and maintains audit processes to ensure compliance with agency procedures and policies.

9. Monitors work flow to avoid delays in processing.

10. Maintains positive relationships with appropriate company representatives through proper contacts and effective communication.

11. Provides assistance to Producers and/or Customer Service Representatives on technical issues when necessary.

12. Maintains control of expirations and renewal processes, ensuring that no accounts are missed.

13. Maintains control over department's non-resident activities and countersignature requirements.

14. Interviews, hires, and terminates department staff to ensure professionalism and a high-level of technical and personal skills.

Page 1 of 3

15. Promotes open communication and high morale.

16. Oversees education, training, and development programs to increase department capability and expertise.

17. Achieves agency goals regarding percentage of retained business.

18. Ensures high levels of customer service and satisfaction by improving ongoing service delivery methods.

19. Facilitates and oversees underwriting standards in department.

20. Maintains a desirable mix of business and aggressively assists CSRs in rounding out the book of business.

21. Keeps informed regarding insurance technical knowledge, market trends, agency automation, company information, and other operating techniques.

22. Oversees the use of excess, surplus market placements to ensure best price and coverage for the client.

23. Documents all material conversations with insureds and/or carrieriers regarding exposures and coverages.

24. Performs other functions as assigned by management.

C. KNOWLEDGE, SKILLS AND ABILITIES

A high level of technical insurance knowledge, be organized, and possess excellent verbal and written communication skills. College degree is desired. At least five years experience in property and casualty underwriting and marketing with a multi-line insurance agency or brokerage operation. Math skills, including the ability to add, subtract, multiply, and divide whole numbers and do calculations involving decimals and fractions

D. OTHER REQUIREMENTS

All licenses as required by the State Department of Insurance to discuss and/or sell insurance in states where the agency functions. Ability to use personal computer, calculator, agency automation system, and various software programs, including but not limited to Microsoft Word and Excel.

E. WORKING CONDITIONS

Fast-paced multi-tasking environment.

F. GENERAL

1. This job description is intended to describe the level of work required of the person performing the job.

2. Essential functions are outlined; other duties may be assigned as needs arise or as required to support the agency's essential functions.

3. This description is not intended as a contract and is subject to unilateral change and revision by management.

4. Any written contractual agreements will supersede this job description.

5. All requirements may be modified to reasonably accommodate physically or mentally challenged employees.

I have read, understand, and agree to abide by the job description.

_____   _____

Signature   Date

Exhibit: Mail / File Clerk Job Description

Mail / File Clerk Job Description

Position Title: Mail / File Clerk

Reports to: _____

Compensation Range: _____ to _____

A. SUMMARY

Maintains hard account files, including scanning, copying, and purging of files. Provides clerical backup/support for receptionist and other clerical staff as needed.

B. POSITION FUNCTIONS

1. Sets up, maintains, and locates files for other agency personnel.

2. Provides miscellaneous clerical backup for administrative staff and receptionist.

3. Photocopies and/or scans items necessary for maintaining files or assisting agency personnel.

4. Purges files annually to remove dead, expired, or canceled files from current file storage systems and stores them in appropriate dead file systems.

5. Prepares all UPS, Certified and Overnight mailings for same-day pickup.

6. Delivers certified mail to Post Office when required.

7. Has responsibility for amount of postage in the metering machine and for advising accounting when funds need to be replenished.

8. Transmits and receives faxes. Delivers or emails incoming faxes to appropriate personnel within one hour of receipt.

9. Opens and distributes all deliveries within four hours of receipt.

10. Performs other functions as assigned by management.

C. KNOWLEDGE, SKILLS AND ABILITIES

Excellent knowledge of alphabetical and numeric sequencing, with ability to communicate effectively with others.

D. OTHER REQUIREMENTS

High School or equivalent with desire to advance in company.

Page 1 of 2

E. WORKING CONDITIONS

Fast-paced multi-tasking environment.

F. GENERAL

1. This job description is intended to describe the level of work required of the person performing the job.

2. Essential functions are outlined; other duties may be assigned as needs arise or as required to support the agency's essential functions.

3. This description is not intended as a contract and is subject to unilateral change and revision by management.

4. Any written contractual agreements will supersede this job description.

5. All requirements may be modified to reasonably accommodate physically or mentally challenged employees.

I have read, understand, and agree to abide by the job description.

_____   _____

Signature   Date

Exhibit: Commercial Marketing Manager Job Description

Commercial Marketing Manager Job Description

Position Title: Commercial Marketing Manager

Reports to: _____

Compensation Range: _____ to _____

A. SUMMARY

Provides direction and assistance to agency personnel for placement of all commercial lines business with awareness of carrier premium volume requirements and commitments.

B. POSITION FUNCTIONS

1. Participates in the discussion and review of the current market situation of specific accounts.

2. Maintains knowledge of current marketplace and capabilities for providing risk placement alternatives.

3. Provides detailed direction for assembling pertinent information necessary for complete applications. Reviews applications for market identification and submission requirements.

4. Performs underwriting functions whenever necessary to make sure classification and rating are complete and accurate.

5. Negotiates pricing, policy conditions, and terms with selected companies. Reviews all quotations with recommendations as to the best options for price, coverage, and risk alternatives.

6. Provides Producer with a complete proposal on each risk accepted and quoted, at least 48 hours prior to appointment.

7. Maintains positive relationships with appropriate company representatives through proper contacts and effective communication.

8. Provides assistance to Producers and Customer Service Representatives when necessary for response to technical issues.

9. Checks new policies for accuracy of all coverages, forms, and premium charges within 24 hours of receipt.

10. Ensures that on all out-of-state business, the writing company is aware of our non-resident and countersignature arrangements in the state where the risk is located.

11. Documents all material conversations with insureds and/or carriers regarding exposures and coverages.

12. Performs other functions as assigned by management.

Page 1 of 2

C. KNOWLEDGE, SKILLS AND ABILITIES

Excellent commercial insurance technical knowledge, including athorough understanding of all forms of commercial coverages and risk alternatives. Outstanding verbal and written communication skills. Able to take initiative, be a self-starter, and influence others.

D. OTHER REQUIREMENTS

College degree or equivalent is desired. Should have at least five years experience in underwriting and marketing with a major insurance company.All licenses to discuss or place insurance as required by the State Department of Insurance in states where the agency functions. Ability to use personal computer, calculator, agency automation systems, and various software programs including but not limited to Microsoft Word and Excel.

E. WORKING CONDITIONS

Fast-paced multi-tasking environment.

F. GENERAL

1. This job description is intended to describe the level of work required of the person performing the job.

2. Essential functions are outlined; other duties may be assigned as needs arise or as required to support the agency's essential functions.

3. This description is not intended as a contract and is subject to unilateral change and revision by management.

4. Any written contractual agreements will supersede this job description.

5. All requirements may be modified to reasonably accommodate physically or mentally challenged employees.

I have read, understand, and agree to abide by the job description.

_____   _____

Signature

Date

Exhibit: Office Manager Job Description

Office Manager Job Description

Position Title: Office Manager

Reports to: _____

Compensation Range: _____ to _____

A. SUMMARY

Is responsible for the communication, interpretation, and administration of policies and procedures. Deals directly with employees and managers on issues concerning benefits, compensation, employee relations, policy and procedure formulation, training and development, incentive plans, and salary administration. Acts as in-house expert on all human resources issues. Manages and develops human resources.

Develops formal training programs designed to provide employees with the skills, knowledge, and tools necessary to attain both department and agency goals. Coordinates and conducts training for the agency.

B. POSITION FUNCTIONS

1. Ensures all employees are complying with agency systems and procedures.

2. Manages and administers agency training programs.

3. Develops workflows and procedures to ensure high-quality service and compliance with agency standards; continuously refines standards, workflows, and procedures.

4. Ensures agency efficiency through continuous process improvement efforts and effective utilization of systems automation implementation.

5. Develops and administers employment policies and procedures and carries out personnel objectives and programs.

6. Communicates all agency issues and acts as intermediary between staff and upper management.

7. Advises senior management on future organization planning and development of select staff members.

8. Acts as in-house expert on all issues relating to human resource functions and knows where to locate available resources.

9. Understands business issues and concerns and how they relate to agency personnel.

10. Maintains current organizational chart and job descriptions.

11. Manages the performance evaluation process so that all employees are evaluated within two weeks of review date.

Page 1 of 3

12. Maintains a current employee handbook in compliance with local, state, and federal laws.

13. Manages labor issues as they arise.

14. Develops and implements the affirmative action program throughout the agency.

15. Manages the areas of compensation planning, wage and salary administration, employee benefits, employee relations, and personnel administration.

16. Oversees the payroll function to ensure that employees are paid accurately and on time.

17. Provides guidance and support to managers on: employment policies; compensation and benefits issues; development and administration of incentive programs; and recruiting.

18. Works with management and staff to identify training needs.

19. Develops training programs, internal and external, to meet needs.

20. Monitors continuing education requirements and industry designation completion, ensuring that all employees satisfy their continuing education requirements on a timely basis.

21. Maintains familiarity with job descriptions and performance reviews to identify and coordinate training requirements.

22. Budgets and monitors training expenses.

23. Performs other duties as requested by management.

C. KNOWLEDGE, SKILLS AND ABILITIES

Excellent understanding of agency workflow and processes. Ability to develop and provide written human resources policies to management and staff. High degree of organization skills required to effectively administer personnel programs, including affirmative action, compensation and benefits, and recruiting; automation system management; training; and corporate planning. Ability to motivate staff and management in maintaining high skill levels.

D. OTHER REQUIREMENTS

College degree, at least a bachelor's level and professional designation, with a minimum of five years' of management experience, preferably in insurance operations. Ability to use personal computer, calculator, agency automation systems and various software programs, including but not limited to Microsoft Word and Excel.

E. WORKING CONDITIONS

Fast-paced, multi-tasking environment.

F. GENERAL

1. This job description is intended to describe the level of work required of the person performing the job.

2. Essential functions are outlined; other duties may be assigned as needs arise or as required to support the agency's essential functions.

3. This description is not intended as a contract and is subject to unilateral change and revision by management.

4. Any written contractual agreements will supersede this job description.

5. All requirements may be modified to reasonably accommodate physically or mentally challenged employees.

I have read, understand, and agree to abide by the job description.

_____   _____

Signature   Date

Exhibit: President Job Description

President Job Description

Position Title: President

Reports to: Board of Directors

Compensation Range: _____ to _____

A. SUMMARY

Assures a profitable agency operation for the stockholders. Maintains a high profile of leadership in the community and the insurance industry. Oversees the daily activities and operations of the corporation.

B. POSITION FUNCTIONS

1. Is responsible for building and developing the agency/corporation strategic business plan.

2. Develops and maintains a professional image of the agency to the public and the insurance industry.

3. Develops and supervises the performance of a strong management team.

4. Reviews all agreements and contracts on behalf of the corporation, whether or not a signature is required.

5. Provides service to selected insurance clients.

6. Makes time available to call on clients with others in the agency when the presence of a corporate officer is necessary or prudent.

7. Performs public relations duties as necessary in the community and the industry.

8. Coordinates a process for the successful, continuous perpetuation of the agency business and ownership.

9. Promotes open communications with all agency personnel to garner and protect high morale.

10. Maintains long-term, high-quality relationships with carriers.

11. Executes and renews all agency contracts; complies with carrier contract; maximizes contingency income.

12. Maintains current knowledge of insurance technical information, market trends, agency systems automation, company underwriting requirements and financial condition, and other operating techniques.

13. Maintains communications with the employees regarding company direction, procedures, training, and other necessary information.

14. Oversees various agency and department meetings.

Page 1 of 2

15. Supports managers in automation and operational research, as well as change requirements and implementation.

16. Participates in projects as assigned by the management committee or the board of directors.

C. KNOWLEDGE, SKILLS AND ABILITIES

Prior experience in a senior management role is desirable. Excellent verbal and written communication skills. Ability to demonstrate strong leadership skills and to create and impart a vision for the future. Exemplify a favorable attitude toward change and continuous improvement as well as commitment to bottom line profit. Understanding of insurance agency operations with agency management experience of no less than five years, including prior experience in business administration.

D. OTHER REQUIREMENTS

College degree or equivalent. Insurance industry knowledge, underwriting or marketing in the property/casualty areas preferred. Ability to communicate effectively at all levels in the organization. Ability to anticipate and avoid problems and capability to solve simple to complex personnel issues. Must have all licenses to discuss or place insurance as required by the State Department of Insurance in states where the agency functions. Ability to use personal computer, calculator, agency automation systems and various software programs, including but not limited to Microsoft Word and Excel.

E. WORKING CONDITIONS

Fast-paced multi-tasking environment.

F. GENERAL

1. This job description is intended to describe the level of work required of the person performing the job.

2. Essential functions are outlined; other duties may be assigned as needs arise or as required to support the agency's essential functions.

3. This description is not intended as a contract and is subject to unilateral change and revision by management.

4. Any written contractual agreements will supersede this job description.

5. All requirements may be modified to reasonably accommodate physically or mentally challenged employees.

I have read, understand, and agree to abide by the job description.

_____   _____

Signature   Date

Page 2 of 2

Exhibit: Sales Manager Job Description

Sales Manager Job Description

Position Title: Sales Manager

Reports To: _____

Compensation Range: _____ to _____

A. SUMMARY

Performs sales and marketing tasks in meeting agency objectives for production and profit. Maintains strong and effective relationships in the business community. Manages and controls the sales operation of the agency. Has authority, overall knowledge of agency operations and insurance knowledge at the management level.

B. POSITION FUNCTIONS

1. Establishes sales goals and plans to assure that each producer contributes to the overall agency objectives. Achieves 100% of annual sales goal.

2. Develops and maintains a comprehensive sales training program to assure meeting agency standards of performance.

3. Conducts annual review for producers including attainment of goals and compensation arrangements. Reviews to occur within 15 days of anniversary date.

4. Coordinates company activities with marketing department to insure compliance with agency agreements.

5. Communicates all systems, procedures, and insurance company regulations to all producers to ensure full compliance.

6. Maintains a recruiting program for selecting and training new producers that will fulfill the overall needs of the agency.

7. Maintains an active and effective role in evaluating and choosing the right companies for the agency.

8. Develops a sales budget to ensure conformity to agency policy on expenses incurred.

9. Plans sales campaigns with carriers and obtains resources from carriers to increase sales effectiveness and profitability of the agency.

10. Works to maintain low loss ratios through loss control practices, implementation of loss reduction programs for clients and utilization of company resources to improve insured's risk management practices, with the outcome being anoverall agency loss ratio not to exceed sixty percent.

Page 1 of 2

11. Maintains excellent relationships with carriers for increased support and the efficient delivery of high-quality products to insureds at fair prices.

12. Documents all material conversations with insureds and/or carriers regarding exposures and coverages.

13. Performs other functions as assigned by management.

C. KNOWLEDGE, SKILLS AND ABILITIES

Prior sales/production management and marketing/underwriting experience with an insurance agency, brokerage firm, or carrier. Innovative, assertive, organized, withexcellent verbal and written communication skills.

D. OTHER REQUIREMENTS

College degree or equivalent. Five plus years insurance industry experience, including underwriting or marketing in the property/casualty areas preferred. All licenses to discuss or place insurance as required by the State Department of Insurance in states where the agency functions. Ability to use personal computer, calculator, agency automation systems and various software programs including but not limited to Microsoft Word and Excel.

E. WORKING CONDITIONS

Fast-paced multi-tasking environment.

F. GENERAL

1. This job description is intended to describe the level of work required of the person performing the job.

2. Essential functions are outlined; other duties may be assigned as needs arise or as required to support the agency's essential functions.

3. This description is not intended as a contract and is subject to unilateral change and revision by management.

4. Any written contractual agreements will supersede this job description.

5. All requirements may be modified to reasonably accommodate physically or mentally challenged employees.

I have read, understand, and agree to abide by the job description.

_____   _____

Signature   Date

Page 2 of 2

Exhibit: CSR Assistant Job Description

CSR Assistant Job Description

Position Title: CSR Assistant

Reports to: _____

Compensation Range: _____ to _____

A. SUMMARY

Assists Customer Service Representatives by processing changes and renewals, by doing rating and/or data entry, making calls to clients or company, or by assisting in any other areas as instructed by the CSR.

B. POSITION FUNCTIONS

1. Maintains files in an orderly, up-to-date manner.

2. Processes change requests for auto and types ID cards on the same day as requested.

3. Processes change confirmations on the same day as requested.

4. Processes confirmed cancellations on the same day as requested.

5. Seeks advice from CSR's with any problem with their accounts.

6. Maintains working knowledge of all company change procedures.

7. Assists or fillsin for Customer Service Representatives as directed.

8. Inputs late-payment notices, direct notice of cancellations, and payment-received notices into the agency automation system.

9. Processes paperwork assigned by Customer Service Representatives on the same day as requested.

10. Maintains working knowledge of all rating products and processes backup rating when needed.

11. Performs other functions as assigned by management.

C. KNOWLEDGE, SKILLS AND ABILITIES

Self-starter, imaginative and creative, with good verbal and written communication skills.

D. OTHER REQUIREMENTS

High school or equivalent degree. Ability to use personal computer, calculator, agency automation systems and various software programs including but not limited to Microsoft Word and Excel.

Page 1 of 2

E. WORKING CONDITIONS

Fast-paced, multi-tasking environment.

F. GENERAL

1. This job description is intended to describe the level of work required of the person performing the job.

2. Essential functions are outlined; other duties may be assigned as needs arise or as required to support the agency's essential functions.

3. This description is not intended as a contract and is subject to unilateral change and revision by management.

4. Any written contractual agreements will supersede this job description.

5. All requirements may be modified to reasonably accommodate physically or mentally challenged employees.

I have read, understand, and agree to abide by the job description.

_____   _____

Signature   Date

Page 2 of 2

Exhibit: Producer Job Description

Producer Job Description

Position Title: Producer

Reports to: _____

Compensation Range: _____ to _____

A. SUMMARY

Sells new accounts and renews existing accounts in keeping with agency and individual goals while building relationships with clients. Identifies and solicits sales prospects from various sources.

B. POSITION FUNCTIONS

1. Presents proposals in a professional manner.

2. Makes the sale and collects necessary deposits, arranges for binders, certificates, etc. Collects all premiums that are due on or before effective date of coverage.

3. Negotiates annual new and renewal production goals with Sales Manager.

4. Develops prospects through an organized agency direct solicitation program, referrals from present accounts, and target-marketing leads and through community affiliations and other contacts.

5. Develops information and recommendations for prospective accounts, presents proposals and adheres to agency policies and procedures for writing a new account.

6. Establishes servicing procedures when necessary for designated accounts.

7. Establishes payment arrangements for each new/renewal account, adhering to agency guidelines, policies and procedures regarding the payment of policy premium.

8. Performs periodic service calls on designated accounts.

9. Maintains a concern for timeliness and completeness when interacting with customers, as well as agency and company personnel, to minimize potentials for error or omission claims.

10. Identifies and solicits sales prospects from various sources provided by agency, by cold calls, mailings, and phone contacts.

11. Solicits referrals from existing agency accounts with a target of an average of two referrals per account annually.

12. Assists in resolving any problems in accounting or claims for accounts produced.

13. Coordinates timely presentations for both new and renewal business.

Page 1 of 2

14. Assists in marketing accounts where appropriate due to relationships or product expertise.

15. Documents all material conversations with insureds and/or carriers regarding exposures and coverages

16. Performs other functions as assigned by management.

C. KNOWLEDGE, SKILLS AND ABILITIES

Aggressive and assertive self-starter with the ability to influence otherswith demonstrated effective verbal and written presentation skills. Willing to travel as required. Expected to meet monthly new business premium goals through a variety of sources: cold calls, referrals, niche marketing, etc.

D. OTHER REQUIREMENTS

Maintains knowledge of underwriting criteria for carriers represented by agency. Assists in collecting earned premiums, audit premiums, etc., when called upon, withany uncollected premiums being the responsibility of the producer. All licenses to discuss or place insurance as required by the State Department of Insurance in states where the agency functions. Ability to use personal computer, calculator, agency automation systems and various software programs, including but not limited to Microsoft Word and Excel.

E. WORKING CONDITIONS

Fast-paced multi-tasking environment.

F. GENERAL

1. This job description is intended to describe the level of work required of the person performing the job.

2. Essential functions are outlined; other duties may be assigned as needs arise or as required to support the agency's essential functions.

3. This description is not intended as a contract and is subject to unilateral change and revision by management.

4. Any written contractual agreements will supersede this job description.

5. All requirements may be modified to reasonably accommodate physically or mentally challenged employees.

I have read, understand, and agree to abide by the job description.

_____   _____

Signature   Date

Exhibit: Receptionist Job Description

Receptionist Job Description

Position Title: Receptionist
Reports to: _____
Compensation Range: _____ to _____

A. SUMMARY

Creates a positive first impression on behalf of the agency. Directs clients to the proper person in a professional, accurate, and timely manner. Performs clerical duties as assigned. Serves as receptionist and point of first contact for all visitors to the office.

B. POSITION FUNCTIONS

1. Acts as office receptionist. Answers calls within three rings.

2. Handles incoming calls in a friendly and courteous manner; provides assistance and information as required and connects caller with desired party.

3. Handles all incoming and outgoing fax messages. Distributes incoming faxes within one hour of receipt.

4. Speaks clearly and uses correct English and proper telephone techniques.

5. Answers client inquiries as possible or directs the inquiry to the person best able to answer the inquiry.

6. Continually checks back with callers on hold to ask if they prefer to continue to hold, leave a message, or be transferred to someone else who can help them.

7. Arranges with telephone company for equipment changes or repairs as directed.

8. Handles all incoming and outgoing Fax messages. Distributes or emails incoming faxes within one hour of receipt.

9. Trains reliefreceptionists.

10. Records and forwards accurate messages including correct name of caller, phone number, and other pertinent information.

11. Performs additional functions as assigned by management.

C. KNOWLEDGE, SKILLS AND ABILITIES

Neat appearance and demonstrates effective telephone etiquette. Friendly, well organized and enjoys dealing with people.

Page 1 of 2

D. OTHER REQUIREMENTS

Prior experience with telephone, as well as high school diploma or equivalent. Ability to use personal computer, calculator, agency automation systems and various software programs, including but not limited to Microsoft Word and Excel.

E. WORKING CONDITIONS

Fast-paced, multi-tasking environment.

F. GENERAL

1. This job description is intended to describe the level of work required of the person performing the job.

2. Essential functions are outlined; other duties may be assigned as needs arise or as required to support the agency's essential functions.

3. This description is not intended as a contract and is subject to unilateral change and revision by management.

4. Any written contractual agreements will supersede this job description.

5. All requirements may be modified to reasonably accommodate physically or mentally challenged employees.

I have read, understand, and agree to abide by the job description.

_____   _____

Signature   Date

Page 2 of 2

Exhibit: Telemarketer Job Description

Telemarketer Job Description

Position Title: Telemarketer

Reports to: _____

Compensation Range: _____ to _____

A. SUMMARY

Performs lead generation and sets sales and service appointments. Makes telephone calls, prepares marketing mailings, and performs computer input and clerical support to the sales processes.

B. POSITION FUNCTIONS

1. Mails one hundred pre-approach letters to prospects per week.

2. Calls one hundred prospects and sets at least ten appointments for producers per week.

3. Sends out follow-up letters and sets follow-up appointments.

4. With guidance of Sales Manager, selects lists of suspects to send pre-approach letters on a weekly basis.

5. Prepares a weekly sales report and reports the results at sales meetings.

6. Prepares log of all pre-approach letters for review by Sales Manager for any necessary changes.

7. Mails and tabulates customer satisfaction surveys.

8. Enters lead lists and individual prospects into agency automation system.

9. Makes cold calls to prospective clients to acquire policy expiration dates and inputs data into agency automation system.

10. Prequalifies prospective sales clients using agency criteria.

11. Tracks and inputs sales, service, and renewal appointments for prospects and current accounts in appropriate information management system.

12. Creates marketing letters and marketing campaigns, and mails information to prospects.

13. Prepares all sales kits to include agency information, necessary applications, brochures, and appropriate special program information upon direction from producers and/or agency management.

14. Performs other functions as assigned by management.

Page 1 of 2

C. KNOWLEDGE, SKILLS AND ABILITIES

Neat appearance, secretarial skills, and good telephone voice. Ability to show initiative and work with minimum supervision. Pleasant, articulate, and willing to make client and prospect contact. High school graduate or college preferred, with background in administrative and business skills.

D. OTHER REQUIREMENTS

Displays excellent telephone etiquette skills. Has ability to use personal computer, calculator, agency automation systems and various software programs, including but not limited to Microsoft Word and Excel.

E. WORKING CONDITIONS

Fast-paced multi-tasking environment.

F. GENERAL

1. This job description is intended to describe the level of work required of the person performing the job.

2. Essential functions are outlined; other duties may be assigned as needs arise or as required to support the agency's essential functions.

3. This description is not intended as a contract and is subject to unilateral change and revision by management.

4. Any written contractual agreements will supersede this job description.

5. All requirements may be modified to reasonably accommodate physically or mentally challenged employees.

I have read, understand, and agree to abide by the job description.

_____   _____

Signature   Date

Section 4: Employee Manual

The Need for an Employee Manual

The Employee Manual is a critical component of the human resources function in an agency. It is an easy and convenient way to make sure that all the employees of the agency know and understand the policies and procedures.

It is also a way for the agency to set ethical and performance-related standards. While you may not be able to force an existing employee to sign a non-piracy or non-compete agreement, you can require all employees to acknowledge and sign for the employee manual.

In the manual you should include wording that addresses the confidential nature of agency information, which is an asset of the agency, and wording that states that employees should not and cannot retain any of this confidential information in the event that they are terminated. Several former employees without separate non-piracy agreements have been successfully sued for breach of confidentiality based upon wording in their employee handbook.

Realize that no manual is better than a "bad" manual. What is a bad manual? Any manual that blatantly violates any federal, state or local human resources law can be considered a bad manual.

For example: A manual that states that the agency is based on a Christian foundation and says that each morning there is a voluntary corporate prayer could be considered a bad manual. The agency owner who used that manual unsuccessfully argued that the prayer was voluntary and therefore not a problem.

Problems arose for that owner when he terminated a recently hired employee who was the only one that declined to participate in the prayer. The agent's argument? That the employee was not working up to his level of satisfaction. The employee's argument? That she was fired because she didn't participate in the "voluntary" corporate prayer.

Just defending a lawsuit like this can cost an agency tens of thousands of dollars. Losing can run into the hundreds of thousands. So how do you determine whether you have a good or bad manual? You don't! And don't use your general counsel. Before implementing an Employee Manual, have it reviewed by a qualified attorney who specializes in employment law.

Once your employment law attorney approves your manual, get each employee to sign for his or her copy of the manual. These acknowledgement forms become part of your documentation and should be kept in a safe place.

But what should be included in the manual? It depends on the size and type of agency as well as the intended scope of the manual. Depending on the number of employees, different human resources laws will be applicable and should be addressed by the manual.

The following is a list of some things that should be included in the employee manual:

Introductory Information

Disclaimer – Every Employee Manual should have a disclaimer stating that the manual is not a contract and that management reserves the right to unilaterally modify it at any time.

Welcome Letter – Should talk about what makes your agency different and how the employee will be part of a team.

Introduction – Should restate that this is not a contract and employment is "at will." If management has an "open door" policy, this is a good place to state it.

Mission Statement – If the agency has developed a mission statement, include it in the manual for reinforcement.

Value Statements – Some of the most important performance standards should be included as value statements.

Organizational Structure – Should describe the agency's organizational structure. If you have multiple locations, say so but don't list the locations or state the specific number of locations. This helps reduce the need for revisions.

Recruitment and Employment

Equal Employment Opportunity – State that you do not discriminate and that you comply with the applicable federal, state, and local laws.

Hiring of Relatives – Many insurance agencies have family members working in the agency. If you have rules against nepotism, say so. If you have family members working at the agency, or if it is likely to occur in the future, leave this section out.

Immigration Law Compliance – Especially in light of September 11, state that you are required to comply with the Immigration Reform and Control Act of 1986 and that employees are required to complete an I-9 form. (See the information under Section 2: Employment Law.)

Conflicts of Interest – You don't want employees making decisions that benefit them while hurting the agency. Explain why employees should disclose potential conflicts of interest.

Confidentiality / Employment Agreement – State that all employees are bound by Confidentiality Agreements they are required to sign. It should also state that even if there is no Confidentiality Agreement, they still cannot reveal agency secrets. If the agency also uses non-piracy and/or non-compete agreements, you may want to reference it here.

Classification of Employees – State what type of employees you have. While you may have temporary employees, you never ever have "permanent" employees. Using such a term could be construed as just that, a permanent employee whom you can never terminate.

Make sure you address the issue of overtime here. Many people are under the misconception that if an employee is paid a salary, he or she is not eligible for overtime. Whether a person is paid hourly or a salary is irrelevant. The determining factor is whether an employee is "exempt" or "non-exempt." (See Fair Labor Standards Act in Section 2: Employment Law.)

Orientation Program – Does the agency have one? If it does, talk about what happens during this time.

Introductory or Probationary Periods – Among human resources professionals, there is some disagreement as to whether or not to have a probationary period. People think that it is easier to terminate someone during a probationary period. In fact, you can terminate anyone, at any time, for any reason, as long as you are not running afoul of any federal, state, or local employment laws. This author's opinion is that an employee's probationary period starts when he is hired and ends when he is terminated. As a result, calling the initial period of employment an "introductory" period is preferable to calling it a "probationary" period.

Employment Application – Require everyone to fully complete an employment application and state that if there is any misrepresentation, you can terminate the employee at any time.

Termination of Employment

Resignation – You can request two weeks' notice from an employee, but you cannot require it. Remember employment is at will.

Dismissal – You may want to list some of the reasons an employee can be terminated.

COBRA – Outline the rights of an employee under COBRA. While this helps communicate the employee's rights, you are still required to give each employee (and his or her spouse, if any) an Initial COBRA Notice at the time coverage under the plan begins, as well as give each qualified beneficiary a COBRA Notification Form upon termination. (See the COBRA information in Section 2: Employment Law.)

Accrued Vacation and Sick Pay – State whether or not a terminating employee is entitled to accrued vacation or sick pay.

Severance Pay – State what policy, if any, the agency has.

Compensation Administration

Payday – State when compensation is paid and what happens if payday falls on a weekend or holiday. Include whether or not the agency offers direct deposit and what deductions, if any, are deducted from a paycheck.

Benefits – You should state who is eligible for benefits and when they become eligible. If you have a Flexible Spending Account, mention it here.

Timekeeping – Discuss why keeping time records is important and what method will be used. You should also state that overtime must be pre-approved by management. Realize that if management knows (or should have known) that employees are working overtime even if it is not approved, the Federal government can require the employer to pay overtime to non-exempt employees since the agency has been unjustly enriched. (See Fair Labor Standards Act in Section 2: Employment Law.)

Evaluation Dates & Review – Outline when an employee should expect to receive a performance evaluation. Make sure to clarify that just because someone is being evaluated does not necessarily mean that there will be an adjustment in compensation.

Certification Bonuses – Employees attaining different certifications benefit both the employee and the agency. Consider recognizing attainment with a bonus.

Recruitment Bonus – Recruiting is expensive, especially if the agency uses a headhunter. Consider paying employees for good referrals who get hired; it's cheaper than paying a recruiter. Employees tend to refer only good candidates; otherwise, it reflects poorly on them.

Scheduling

Holidays – Outline what days the agency recognizes as holidays and what happens if the holiday falls on a weekend. State which employees receive holiday pay (salary and/or hourly, part-time and/or full-time.)

Vacations – Discuss how many vacation days an employee is entitled to. Be careful when discussing how vacation is calculated. If you state that after one year of employment an employee is entitled to 5 days vacation, the employee fully vests in the 5 days after completing one year of employment.

On the other hand, you may want the employee to accrue vacation on a monthly basis. If an employee starts accruing at a rate of 0.8333 days per month (10 days a year,) and only works for six months, he is only entitled to 5 days of vacation that year. If he used more than 5 days when he terminates after six months, you can deduct the excess vacation from his final paycheck. Remember, though, that some states require that such a deduction be authorized in writing by the employee. Make sure you state whether or not vacation can be taken prior to being earned and if vacation is calculated on a calendar or anniversary basis.

You should also state whether or not vacation days can accrue from year-to-year.

Personal (Sick) Days – As you did with vacation, determine if personal days vest at one time or are accrued month-by-month. State whether and when you will require a physician's statement and if personal days can accrue year-to-year. Consider paying money or comp days for perfect attendance, or buying back unused personal days.

Military Leave – Make a statement regarding your policy on military leave, making sure you comply with the Uniformed Services Employment & Reemployment Rights Act.

Bereavement Leave – Outline how many days off an employee is entitled to take for a death in the family and define who is a member of the family.

Jury Duty – State your Jury Duty policy. While you can limit the number of paid jury duty leave days, you cannot limit the number of unpaid jury duty leave days. Make sure you are in compliance with the Jury System Improvement Act. (See Section 2: Employment Law.)

General Information

Absentee Records – State who maintains them.

Accidents – Explain your process for reporting an accident?

Automation System – Discuss passwords and what information should be input into the system.

Business Travel – Discuss the approval process for hotels and/or airfares as well as the policy regarding taking spouses on trips.

Complaint Procedure – If there is a problem, what is the process to address that complaint?

Desk Audits – State your position that management reserves the right to search an employee's desk as well as other property and equipment supplied by the agency.

Discipline – Address how corrective measures are taken.

Dress Standards – Outline what is and is not considered appropriate behavior and dress. You may want to include a discussion about tattoos and/or piercing in this section but be cognizant of any potential religious implications of the tattoos or piercings. These, as well as dress standards, could turn into a freedom of religion issue. If you have a casual day, mention it here.

Drug-Free Workplace – Discuss the fact that alcohol and controlled substances are not to be used or brought to the worksite and what happens if an employee is caught on your premises, and/or if convicted of using illegal drugs.

Educational Assistance – Does the agency pay up front for classes, or reimburse the employee only after passing the class? What courses qualify for reimbursement? Does this apply to all employees or just certain classes of employees (e.g., just producers?)?

Email & Internet Usage – State that the email and Internet systems are not for personal use and the agency reserves the right to read all incoming or outgoing emails.

Employee Personnel Records System – Address who keeps it, what is in it, and the employee's responsibility to notify management of relevant changes (e.g., name, address, marital status).

Employment Reference Checks – State what information, if any, you will provide to potential future employers on current or past employees.

Employee Solicitations – Employees soliciting other employees for fundraisers, subscriptions, etc can waste significant time and energy. Additionally, solicited employees may feel awkward or uncomfortable. Discuss what the policy of the agency is in this section, taking care to avoid violating the National Labor Relations Act which allows employees to engage in "concerted activity."

Expense Report Policy – When is it due, what is the appropriate form, when are receipts required, and when is reimbursement made?

Harassment Policy – Explain what types of harassment there are and why harassment is inappropriate in the workplace. You also need to tell employees what the process / procedure is for reporting harassment, being sure to provide more than one person to whom complaints can be directed. Mention confidentiality and prohibit retaliation. Failure to include this in an employee manual could result in a significant employment practices liability claim.

Leaves of Absence – If the agency is covered by the Family and Medical Leave Act, make sure that the leave of absence policy is in compliance with the FMLA. (See Section 2: Employment Law.)

Life-Threatening Illnesses – Address the fact that medical information is kept confidential and that the employee will not lose his job unless he cannot perform the functions of the job.

Mail – State that the postage machine is not to be used for personal use.

Non-Smoking Policy – If you have a smoke-free workplace, say so. Just because an employee smokes, you are not required to provide him or her with a smoke break. If you do, then you will have to provide the non-smokers with a break as well.

Office Appearance – Indicate that is it everyone's responsibility to keep the office neat and clean and to make sure confidential information is stored securely.

Outside Employment – Address conflicts of interest as well as what happens if an outside job interferes with the employee's ability to perform satisfactorily.

Security Inspections – The work environment should be free of drugs, guns, and other improper material. Searches of company property can be conducted at any time without notice. If employees don't want management to find something, they shouldn't bring it to the office. This can also be reinforced in the Workplace Searches section.

Telephone Etiquette – Mention how the telephone should be answered in a professional and courteous manner within three rings. You should also include the agency's goal in regard to returning calls (e.g., by the end of the business day), and anything that must be included in voice mail messages (such as not being able to bind coverage via voice mail).

Employee Manual Acknowledgement – The employee should acknowledge, in writing, that he has received the employee manual and agrees to abide by it. If the manual is not printed but available on the computer instead, you should still get a written acknowledgement.

If the manual is online, replace the first sentence of Acknowledgement paragraph on the last page of the following manual with:

> I acknowledge that I have received instructions on how to access the **<ENTER AGENCY NAME>** Employee Manual on the computer system.

Sample Employee Manual

The following is a sample employee manual. Before using it in your agency you should do the following:

Replace **<ENTER AGENCY NAME>** with the name of your agency.

Read it carefully, word for word, and edit it so it says what you want it to say. If you fail to do this, implementation of the manual may cause you more harm than good.

Spend some money and have it reviewed by an employment law attorney to make sure that it is in compliance with all applicable federal, state, and local laws.

After you have done all of the above, distribute it to all current and future employees and have them sign a form acknowledging their receipt and agreement to abide by the manual.

Exhibit: Employee Manual

DISCLAIMER

This manual is not a contract, express or implied, guaranteeing employment for any specific duration. Although we hope that your employment relationship with us will be long-term, either you or **<ENTER AGENCY NAME>** may terminate this relationship at any time, for any reason, with or without cause or notice.

<ENTER AGENCY NAME> reserves the right to revise, supplement, or rescind any portion of this manual at any time as it deems appropriate in its sole and absolute discretion.

Please understand that no supervisor, manager, or representative of **<ENTER AGENCY NAME>**, other than the President, has the authority to enter into any agreement with you for employment for any specified period or to make any promises or commitments contrary to the foregoing. Further, any employment agreement entered into by the President shall not be enforceable unless it is in writing.

TABLE OF CONTENTS

WELCOME!

Welcome to **<ENTER AGENCY NAME>**

You have been carefully chosen to be a member of the exciting, dynamic, and growing team that is **<ENTER AGENCY NAME>**. Please remember that each of you is **<ENTER AGENCY NAME>** to our clients. How you think, speak, dress, act, and present yourself is what our clients believe **<ENTER AGENCY NAME>** to be.

- A courteous telephone style makes a difference.

- Staying an extra five minutes to get a quote completed makes a difference.

- Editing every letter or proposal for clarity and spelling makes a difference.

There is an endless list of examples of extra qualities, which an **<ENTER AGENCY NAME>** employee could possess.

We have assembled a unique, dynamic and hard-working team to serve our growing clientele. You will be expected to respond positively to changing circumstances as the needs of clients evolve.

Working at **<ENTER AGENCY NAME>** is demanding, rewarding and challenging. You should gain a sense of satisfaction from being a member of a most responsive, innovative and client dedicated team.

This employee manual is your personal reference to the policies and practices of our firm. In designing our manual, we have attempted to balance our goals with the importance of meeting your basic needs of good working conditions and a sense of accomplishment in your work.

It is our hope that, through a better understanding of **<ENTER AGENCY NAME>** and its programs, you will be able to align your personal goals with those of **<ENTER AGENCY NAME>**. In doing so, we can all succeed together. This creates a win-win situation.

Sincerely,

<PRESIDENT'S NAME>
President, **<ENTER AGENCY NAME>**

INTRODUCTION

This manual serves as a source of information for employees regarding the policies and procedures of **<ENTER AGENCY NAME>**. It provides important information concerning your relationship to the organization, as well as an explanation of pay and benefit programs. If, after you read this manual, you have any questions, or would like to have a further explanation of any policies, you are invited to contact your supervisor. Since it is impossible to cover every situation, policy, rule and interpretation in a manual, what is covered is felt to be information which would be of most frequent interest to you, as an employee of **<ENTER AGENCY NAME>**.

The provisions of this Employee Manual are not intended to, and shall never be construed as, stating the terms and conditions of your employment or providing any contractual rights or guarantees of employment of any kind or nature whatsoever. In consideration of your employment by **<ENTER AGENCY NAME>**, you agree to conform to the rules and regulations of **<ENTER AGENCY NAME>**, and you expressly understand and agree that your employment and compensation can be terminated with or without cause, and with or without notice, at any time, at the option of either **<ENTER AGENCY NAME>** or yourself. You further understand that no manager or representative of **<ENTER AGENCY NAME>** other than the President has any authority to enter into any agreement for employment for any specified period of time, or to make any agreement with you contrary to the foregoing.

<ENTER AGENCY NAME> is a professional organization dedicated to providing the best insurance products available to its clients at the most economical cost.

<ENTER AGENCY NAME> is dedicated to the achievement of success. To our agency, success is:

- Operating profitably through the growth of income and the control of expenses.

- Providing our clients with the best insurance products available in the marketplace, at the best possible price.

- Providing our clients with prompt, accurate and courteous service at all times.

The success of our agency depends upon the sum total of our individual efforts, working together.

In order to achieve that goal, we must constantly establish, monitor and meet objectives. The basis for establishing these objectives must come from an analysis of the facts. We must closely analyze present and past situations to decide what phases of our operations are satisfactory, and also where improvements can be made.

We believe all employees should be well-informed. If at any time you have questions about your employment with us that are not covered in this manual, just ask your supervisor. It is important to know that your supervisor is your best source of information with **<ENTER AGENCY NAME>** and is always willing to take time to help you.

MISSION STATEMENT

VALUE STATEMENTS

- Phone calls must always be returned within 24 hours.

- Audits, binders and certificates must always be processed within 24 hours.

- Claims will always be processed within 24 hours.

- We will promote from within whenever possible.

- We will always ask for referrals.

- We will always maintain corporate financial integrity.

- We will always maintain client confidentiality.

- Every employee will always be a sales person.

- We will not knowingly misrepresent data to any carrier.

- We will support the ongoing development of all employees through education and training.

ORGANIZATIONAL STRUCTURE

<ENTER AGENCY NAME> is a corporation that owns insurance agencies in many locations. This allows **<ENTER AGENCY NAME>** to achieve certain economies through premium writings, commissions, contingencies, and expenses. Although you are working at a specific agency branch, you are an employee of the **<ENTER AGENCY NAME>** corporation. At times, you may be asked to assist another **<ENTER AGENCY NAME>** office.

PEOPLE are our most important asset. In order to attain the greatest utilization of this asset, it is necessary to establish a solid organizational structure.

In establishing our organizational structure the following five criteria exist:

1. **Strong Lines of Supervision** - We must ensure that all employees have one and only one manager. We consider this of utmost importance for not only **<ENTER AGENCY NAME>** but for the employees as well.

2. **Centralized Processing Functions** - We must ensure all functions in our organization are defined and that employees are specifically assigned and expertly trained in the performance of these functions. We also must ensure that all work for these functions is performed by the employees assigned the responsibility.

3. **Workload Accountability** - We must maintain records regarding the amount of incoming work received by the agency, each department, and each employee so workload is evenly distributed and bottlenecks do not occur in the flow of work through our agency. We must also, on a weekly basis, take an "inventory" of unprocessed transactions so management will know where workflow problems exist.

4. **Workflow Accountability** - We must communicate to management on a weekly basis, information about the amount of incoming work and unprocessed work so management can react to problems before they become crises.

5. **Growth Potential** - We must have an organizational structure where we can easily add people as we grow so the entire structure does not have to be changed when there are increases in sales which will, in turn, increase workload.

Organization begins with the assignment of responsibilities to each of you. Once you have been assigned a position classification, you will be expected to perform all job-related responsibilities to the best of your ability.

You will be told what your responsibilities are, both orally and in writing. It is your responsibility to ask questions if there is anything you do not understand about your job.

You will occasionally be asked to act as a coordinator for projects delegated by management.

You will be asked to set career goals with your supervisor annually, teach your responsibilities to employees in training, and assist management in monitoring the workload balance.

There is a great deal of importance placed on the assignment of job responsibilities. You will also be assigned responsibilities you will automatically assume in the absence of a fellow worker. You will become a "back up" for another person in the event of their sickness, vacation, etc. Your secondary responsibilities will be explained to you at the time your primary responsibilities are assigned.

We must each make an effort to review our job descriptions periodically and change them as growth necessitates.

RECRUITMENT AND TERMINATION

EQUAL EMPLOYMENT OPPORTUNITY

<ENTER AGENCY NAME> provides equal employment opportunities to all employees and applicants for employment without regard to race, color, religion, sex, national origin, age, sexual orientation, disability, or veteran status in accordance with applicable federal laws. In addition, **<ENTER AGENCY NAME>** complies with applicable state and local laws governing nondiscrimination in employment in every location in which **<ENTER AGENCY NAME>** has facilities. This policy applies to all terms and conditions of employment, including but not limited to, hiring, placement, promotion, termination, layoff, recall, transfer, leaves of absence, compensation, and training.

<ENTER AGENCY NAME> expressly prohibits any form of unlawful employee harassment based on race, color, religion, sex, national origin, age, sexual orientation, disability, veteran status, or status in any group protected by federal, state or local law. Improper interference with the ability of **<ENTER AGENCY NAME>**'s employees to perform their expected job duties is not tolerated.

HIRING OF RELATIVES

The employment of relatives in the same area of an organization may cause serious conflicts and problems with favoritism and employee morale. In addition to claims of partiality in treatment at work, personal conflicts from outside the work environment can be carried into day-to-day working relationships.

Although **<ENTER AGENCY NAME>** has no prohibition against hiring relatives of existing employees, we will rarely allow relatives to work in the same office. In case of actual or potential problems, **<ENTER AGENCY NAME>** will take prompt action. This can include reassignment or, if necessary, termination of employment for one or both of the individuals involved.

For the purposes of this policy, a relative is any person who is related by blood or marriage, or whose relationship with the employee is similar to that of persons who are related by blood or marriage.

EMPLOYMENT REFERENCE CHECKS

To ensure that individuals who join **<ENTER AGENCY NAME>** are well-qualified and have a strong potential to be productive and successful, it is the policy of **<ENTER AGENCY NAME>** to check the employment references of all applicants.

<ENTER AGENCY NAME> will respond in writing only to those reference check inquiries that are submitted in writing. Responses to such inquiries will confirm only dates of employment, wage rates, and position(s) held. No other employment data will be released without a written authorization and release signed by the individual who is the subject of the inquiry.

IMMIGRATION LAW COMPLIANCE

<ENTER AGENCY NAME> is committed to employing only United States citizens and aliens who are authorized to work in the United States and does not unlawfully discriminate on the basis of citizenship or national origin.

In compliance with the Immigration Reform and Control Act of 1986, each new employee, as a condition of employment, must complete the Employment Eligibility Verification Form I-9 and present documentation establishing identity and employment eligibility. Former employees who are rehired must also complete the form if they have not completed an I-9 with **<ENTER AGENCY NAME>** within the past three years, or if their previous I-9 is no longer retained or valid.

CONFLICTS OF INTEREST

Employees have an obligation to conduct business within guidelines that prohibit actual or potential conflicts of interest. This policy establishes only the framework within which **<ENTER AGENCY NAME>** wishes the business to operate. The purpose of these guidelines is to provide general direction so that employees can seek further clarification on issues related to the subject of acceptable standards of operation. Contact the Operations Manager for more information or questions about conflicts of interest.

Page 8 of 36

Transactions with outside firms must be conducted within a framework established and controlled by the executive level of **<ENTER AGENCY NAME>**. Business dealings with outside firms should not result in unusual gains for those firms. Unusual gain refers to bribes, product bonuses, special fringe benefits, unusual price breaks, and other windfalls designed to ultimately benefit the employer, the employee, or both. Promotional plans that could be interpreted to involve unusual gain require specific executive level approval.

An actual or potential conflict of interest occurs when an employee is in a position to influence a decision that may result in a personal gain for that employee or for a relative as a result of **<ENTER AGENCY NAME>**'s business dealings. For the purposes of this policy, a relative is any person who is related by blood or marriage, or whose relationship with the employee is similar to that of persons who are related by blood or marriage.

No "presumption of guilt" is created by the mere existence of a relationship with outside firms. However, if employees have any influence on transactions involving purchases, contracts, or leases, it is imperative that they disclose to an officer of **<ENTER AGENCY NAME>** as soon as possible the existence of any actual or potential conflict of interest so that safeguards can be established to protect all parties.

Personal gain may result not only in cases where an employee or relative has a significant ownership in a firm with which **<ENTER AGENCY NAME>** does business, but also when an employee or relative receives any kickback, bribe, substantial gift, or special consideration as a result of any transaction or business dealings involving **<ENTER AGENCY NAME>**.

TESTING

In cases where testing is done prior to employment, the purpose, nature, and performance standards of the test are explained to the candidate.

CONFIDENTIALITY / EMPLOYMENT AGREEMENT

Everyone employed by **<ENTER AGENCY NAME>** is required to sign a confidentiality agreement. When an employee signs the agreement, he/she is agreeing not to reveal any confidential information belonging to the agency or its customers to any person, firm, corporation, or association, both during and after the term of employment. Even without such agreement, all members of the staff are bound by this confidentiality.

Employees may also be required to sign an agreement not to compete with **<ENTER AGENCY NAME>** in specific ways and/or solicit **<ENTER AGENCY NAME>** clients for a specific period of time after leaving **<ENTER AGENCY NAME>**.

JOB OPPORTUNITY POSTING

It is the policy of **<ENTER AGENCY NAME>** to make employees aware of job opportunities within the agency. Generally, job opportunities below the management level are posted on designated bulletin boards in each location.

CLASSIFICATIONS OF EMPLOYMENT

For purposes of salary administration and eligibility for overtime payments and employee benefits, **<ENTER AGENCY NAME>** classifies its employees as follows:

Full-time regular employees. Employees hired to work **<ENTER AGENCY NAME>**'s normal, full-time, 40-hour workweek on a regular basis. Such employees may be "exempt" or "nonexempt" as defined below.

Part-time regular employees. Employees hired to work fewer than 40 hours per week on a regular basis. Such employees may be "exempt" or "nonexempt" as defined below.

Temporary employees. Employees engaged to work full-time or part-time on **<ENTER AGENCY NAME>**'s payroll with the understanding that their employment will be terminated no later than on completion of a specific assignment or the end of a specified term or season. (Note that a temporary employee may be offered and may accept a new temporary assignment with **<ENTER AGENCY NAME>** and thus still retain temporary status.) Such employees may be "exempt" or "nonexempt" as defined below. (Employees hired from temporary employment agencies for specific assignments are employees of the respective agency and not of **<ENTER AGENCY NAME>**.)

Leased Workers. Workers assigned to work at **<ENTER AGENCY NAME>** through a leasing organization. Leased workers may be "exempt" or "nonexempt" as defined below. Leased workers are employees of the leasing organization and not of **<ENTER AGENCY NAME>**.

Nonexempt employees. Employees who are required to be paid overtime under the specific provisions of federal and state wage and hour laws.

Exempt employees. Employees who are not required to be paid overtime, in accordance with applicable federal and state wage and hour laws, for work performed beyond 40 hours in a workweek. Executives, professional employees, outside sales representatives, and certain employees in administrative positions are typically exempt.

You will be informed of your initial employment classification as an exempt or nonexempt employee during your orientation session. If you change positions during your employment as a result of a promotion, transfer, or otherwise, you will be informed by the Operations Manager of any change in your exemption status.

Please direct any questions regarding your employment classification or exemption status to the Operations Manager.

ORIENTATION PROGRAM

During your first few days of employment, you will participate in an orientation program conducted by the Operations Manager and various members of your department, including your supervisor. During this program, you will receive important information regarding the performance requirements of your position, basic **<ENTER AGENCY NAME>** policies, your compensation, and benefit programs, plus other information necessary to acquaint you with your job and **<ENTER AGENCY NAME>**. You will also be asked to complete all necessary

Page 10 of 36

paperwork at this time, such as medical benefits plan enrollment forms, beneficiary designation forms, and appropriate federal, state, and local tax forms. At this time, you will be required to present **<ENTER AGENCY NAME>** with information establishing your identity and your eligibility to work in the United States in accordance with applicable federal law.

Please use this orientation program to familiarize yourself with **<ENTER AGENCY NAME>**, our policies and benefits. We encourage you to ask any questions you may have during this program so that you will understand all the guidelines that affect and govern your employment relationship with us.

INTRODUCTORY PERIODS

The introductory period is intended to give new employees the opportunity to demonstrate their ability to achieve a satisfactory level of performance and to determine whether the new position meets their expectations. **<ENTER AGENCY NAME>** uses this period to evaluate employee capabilities, work habits, and overall performance. Either the employee or **<ENTER AGENCY NAME>** may end the employment relationship at will at any time during or after the introductory period, with or without cause or advance notice.

All new and rehired employees work on an introductory basis for the first 90 calendar days after their date of hire. Any significant absence will automatically extend an introductory period by the length of the absence. If **<ENTER AGENCY NAME>** determines that the designated introductory period does not allow sufficient time to thoroughly evaluate the employee's performance, the introductory period may be extended for a specified period.

Upon satisfactory completion of the introductory period, employees enter the "regular" employment classification.

During the introductory period, new employees are eligible for those benefits that are required by law, such as workers' compensation insurance and Social Security. After becoming regular employees, they may also be eligible for other **<ENTER AGENCY NAME>** provided benefits, subject to the terms and conditions of each benefits program. Employees should read the information for each specific benefits program for the details on eligibility requirements.

EMPLOYMENT APPLICATIONS

<ENTER AGENCY NAME> relies upon the accuracy of information contained in the employment application, as well as the accuracy of other data presented throughout the hiring process and employment. Any misrepresentations, falsifications, or material omissions in any of this information or data may result in **<ENTER AGENCY NAME>**'s exclusion of the individual from further consideration for employment or, if the person has been hired, termination of employment.

TRANSFERS

Employees wishing to transfer to other **<ENTER AGENCY NAME>** offices should make their requests in writing to the Operations Manager.

TERMINATION OF EMPLOYMENT

RESIGNATION

It is essential to **<ENTER AGENCY NAME>** and its employees that resignation procedures are followed in order to facilitate replacement, to complete employment records, and to protect employee rights.

<ENTER AGENCY NAME> requests all personnel give an advanced written notice of at least two weeks. The written notice should be given to the employee's supervisor and a copy to the Operations Manager. Taking accrued vacation is not considered part of the resignation notice.

DISMISSAL

The agency reserves the right to discharge employees at will (employees who are not working under a contract for a specified term) at any time. Some, but not all, of the reasons for immediate termination without notice include:

- Unsatisfactory job performance
- Intoxication or use of illegal drugs
- Theft of office equipment or supplies
- Falsifying records
- Breaching client confidentiality
- Insubordination
- Failure to report to work without notice
- Habitual tardiness
- Improper conduct
- Excessive absenteeism
- Conflict of interest

The agency will schedule exit interviews for terminating employees. The exit interview will afford an opportunity to discuss such issues as employee benefits, insurance conversion privileges, compensation, and any other items of information that may be needed for your personnel file. Suggestions, complaints, and questions can also be voiced. Additionally, you are required to return any agency-owned property issued to you during your term of employment.

COBRA

If you resign or are terminated from **<ENTER AGENCY NAME>**'s employ or if your work hours are reduced, and if this event makes you or your dependents no longer eligible to participate in one of our group health insurance plans, you and your eligible dependents may have the right to continue to participate for up to 18 months at your (or your dependents') expense. If it is determined that you qualify as disabled under the Social Security Act within the first 60 days of your COBRA coverage, you may be entitled to continuation coverage for up to 29 months.

Your eligible dependents may also extend coverage, at their expense, for up to 36 months in our group health insurance plans in the event of your death, divorce, legal separation, or enrollment for Medicare benefits, or when a child ceases to be eligible for coverage as a dependent under the terms of the plan. The 18-month continuation coverage period provided in the event of your termination or reduction in working hours may be extended to 36 months for your spouse and dependent children if, within that 18-month period, you die or become divorced or legally separated, or if a child ceases to have dependent status. In addition, if you enroll in Medicare during the 18-month period, your spouse and dependent children may be entitled to extend their continuation period to 36 months, starting on the date that you become eligible for Medicare.

If you or your eligible dependents elect to continue as members of **<ENTER AGENCY NAME>**'s plans, you will be charged the applicable premium charged **<ENTER AGENCY NAME>** by our carriers plus an additional 2 percent. The premium is subject to change if the rates being charged **<ENTER AGENCY NAME>** increase or decrease.

Continuation of coverage may end, however, if any of the following events occur: (1) failure to make timely payments of all premiums; (2) assumption of coverage under another group health plan, which does not exclude or limit coverage to you on account of a preexisting medical condition; or (3) **<ENTER AGENCY NAME>**'s termination of its group health plans. If you enroll for Medicare, you will no longer be eligible for continued coverage, but, as noted earlier in this statement, your spouse and dependent children may be entitled to extend their continuation period.

Our plan administrator will contact you concerning these options at the time termination occurs or your work hours are reduced. The plan administrator will contact your qualified beneficiaries in the event of your death or enrollment for Medicare benefits. However, in the event that you become divorced or legally separated, or one of your dependents ceases to be eligible for coverage under our group health insurance plans, you and/or your dependent are responsible for contacting the plan administrator to discuss continuation/conversion rights. You and your qualified beneficiaries are also responsible for notifying the plan administrator within 60 days of qualifying for Social Security disability benefits.

For further details regarding continuing or converting your group health insurance benefits, please contact the Operations Manager.

ACCRUED VACATION PAY

No employees terminating employment for any reason are entitled to payment for accrued unused vacation time.

ACCRUED SICK PAY

Employees terminating employment for any reason are not entitled to payment for any accrued unused sick time.

SEVERANCE PAY

An employee discharged for cause or terminating voluntarily shall be given no severance pay. Any employee discharged for other than cause may be given severance pay at the discretion of the **<ENTER AGENCY NAME>** President.

Page 13 of 36

LETTERS OF RECOMMENDATION

Work-related letters and / or oral recommendations or references may only be issued by the Operations Manager. Any such communications will merely indicate the first and last days of work and the position(s) held. No other employee may give a work reference on a current or former employee. This policy will not prohibit an employee from providing a character or personal reference.

COMPENSATION ADMINISTRATION

<ENTER AGENCY NAME>'s policy is to attract and retain qualified employees to achieve maximum results per compensation dollar. We include all salaried and hourly non-producer employees in this formalized program. This will allow their compensation to grow commensurate with their worth to **<ENTER AGENCY NAME>**.

The compensation program is a guide to assist **<ENTER AGENCY NAME>** in administering compensation for our support staff. It is not a collection of rules and formulas to be mechanically applied. Instead, it reflects policies and guidelines and contains procedures that serve as a foundation for managerial decision-making in the area of compensation. It is part of an interactive management process that includes the Evaluation Performance Review, Position Descriptions, Counseling Statements, and other programs.

Employees should understand that the program is continually updated so compensation will be commensurate with both the responsibilities of the position and the performance of the individual employee.

COMPENSATION CLASSIFICATIONS

Each position in **<ENTER AGENCY NAME>** has been classified based upon the complexity of the work performed, the value of the position to **<ENTER AGENCY NAME>**, and the relationship of the position to other jobs in **<ENTER AGENCY NAME>**.

An employee's performance will determine where his/her actual compensation falls within the range, and the size and frequency of increases.
Classifications and compensation ranges are periodically reviewed and adjusted to correspond with living costs and conditions in the insurance field.

PAYDAY

All employees are paid semimonthly on the 15th and last day of the month. Each paycheck will include earnings for all work performed through the payroll cutoff date.

In the event that a regularly scheduled payday falls on a day off such as a weekend or holiday, employees will receive pay on the last day of work before the regularly scheduled payday.

If a regular payday falls during an employee's vacation, the employee's paycheck will be available upon his or her return from vacation.

Employees may have pay directly deposited into their bank accounts if they provide advance written authorization to **<ENTER AGENCY NAME>**. Employees will receive an itemized statement of wages when **<ENTER AGENCY NAME>** makes direct deposits.

New Employees: Will receive their check on the scheduled payday for all days worked during the first pay period through the payroll cutoff date.

Terminating Employees: Will receive their final check on the next scheduled payday.

The following deductions are withheld from each paycheck:
1. Social Security (FICA)
2. Federal Income Tax
3. State Income Tax (where applicable)
4. Health Insurance (when applicable)
5. Other benefits (when applicable)

SOCIAL SECURITY (FICA)

Employees and **<ENTER AGENCY NAME>** contribute equal amounts to this federal government program, which provides for retirement income and medical needs. Included in the program is a provision for dependents in the case of disability or death of the covered employee.

BENEFITS

Benefits eligibility is dependent upon a variety of factors, including employee classification. The Operations Manager can identify the programs for which you are eligible.

Only full-time regular employees are eligible for these benefits.

The following sections highlight some of the key points of the benefits available. Refer to the actual plan documents for coverage descriptions and details.

HEALTH INSURANCE

Employees are eligible for health insurance coverage on the first of the month following 90 days of employment. **<ENTER AGENCY NAME>** will pay one-half of the employee's premium. Employees are responsible for the other one-half and 100% of the spouse and dependent premiums. Employees may pay their premium through our Flexible Spending Account plan, thereby paying with "pre-tax" rather than "after-tax" dollars.

The health insurance plan includes $10,000 of life insurance coverage on the employee. The plan also includes an accidental death and dismemberment provision.

For benefit details, please contact our life and health division.

DENTAL COVERAGE

Voluntary dental coverage is available. Employees are eligible for dental coverage on the first of the month following 90 days of employment. For benefit details, please contact our life and health division.

TIMEKEEPING

Accurately recording time worked is the responsibility of every nonexempt employee. Federal and state laws require **<ENTER AGENCY NAME>** to keep an accurate record of time worked in order to calculate employee pay and benefits. Time worked is the time actually spent on the job performing assigned duties.

Nonexempt employees should accurately record the time they begin and end their work, as well as the beginning and ending time of each meal period. They should also record the beginning and ending time of any split shift or departure from work for personal reasons.

Overtime work must always be approved before it is performed. Altering, falsifying, tampering with time records, or recording time on another employee's time record may result in disciplinary action, up to and including termination of employment.

LUNCH PERIOD

Employees are allowed thirty minutes for lunch each day. The Operations Manager schedules lunch periods.

EVALUATION DATES

All employees are evaluated annually and within 30 days of their anniversary date. New employees and employees new to a position will also be evaluated periodically during the initial three-month period.

EVALUATION PERFORMANCE REVIEW

Supervisors and employees are strongly encouraged to discuss job performance and goals on an informal, day-to-day basis. A formal written performance evaluation will be conducted at the end of an employee's initial period of hire, known as the introductory period. Additional formal performance evaluations are conducted to provide both supervisors and employees the opportunity to discuss job tasks, identify and correct weaknesses, encourage and recognize strengths, and discuss positive, purposeful approaches for meeting goals.

Performance evaluations are scheduled approximately every 12 months, coinciding generally with the anniversary of the employee's original regular employee status date (which is 90 days after original hire date).

Merit-based pay adjustments are awarded by **<ENTER AGENCY NAME>** in an effort to recognize truly superior employee performance. The decision to award such an adjustment is dependent upon numerous factors, including the information documented by this formal performance evaluation process.

PROMOTIONAL INCREASES

When an employee receives new or additional responsibilities and / or additional duties that result in promotion, the employee may receive a new compensation classification.

CERTIFICATION BONUSES

There are several professional designations that **<ENTER AGENCY NAME>** believes its employees should strive toward. To motivate our employees, **<ENTER AGENCY NAME>** will reward employees with certification bonuses when they receive the following designations:

CIC - Certified Insurance Counselor	$500
CPCU - Certified Property/Casualty Underwriter	$500
CSP - Certified Safety Professional	$250
ARM - Associate Risk Manager	$250
AIC - Associate in Claims	$250
CISR - Certified Insurance Service Representative	$100
ACSR - Agency Customer Service Representative	$100

New or existing employees already possessing these designations are not eligible for these bonuses.

RECRUITMENT BONUS

We encourage employees to recommend qualified candidates for position openings at **<ENTER AGENCY NAME>** offices. If an employee refers a candidate, a bonus of $500 is paid after a new recruit completes six months of employment with **<ENTER AGENCY NAME>**.

The hiring supervisor is not eligible to receive a recruitment bonus for any candidate.

This bonus is not applicable to or for current employees transferring to other **<ENTER AGENCY NAME>** offices.

SCHEDULING

WORK SCHEDULE

The normal work schedule for all employees is eight hours a day, five days a week. Your supervisor will advise you of the times yours schedule will normally begin and end. Staffing needs and operational demands may necessitate variations in starting and ending times, as well as variations in the total hours that may be scheduled each day and week. Office hours are 9am – 5pm, Monday through Friday.

HOLIDAYS

<ENTER AGENCY NAME> will grant holiday time off to all employees on the holidays listed below.

New Year's Day (January 1)
Memorial Day (last Monday in May)
Independence Day (July 4)
Labor Day (first Monday in September)
Thanksgiving (fourth Thursday in November)
Christmas (December 25)

<ENTER AGENCY NAME> will grant paid holiday time off to all eligible employees who have completed 90 calendar days of service in an eligible employment classification. Holiday pay will be calculated based on the employee's straight-time pay rate (as of the date of the holiday) times the number of hours the employee would otherwise have worked on that day. Only regular full-time employees are eligible.

A recognized holiday that falls on a Saturday will be observed on the preceding Friday. A recognized holiday that falls on a Sunday will be observed on the following Monday.

If a recognized holiday falls during an eligible employee's paid absence (such as vacation or sick leave), holiday pay will be provided instead of the paid time off benefit that would otherwise have applied.

If eligible nonexempt employees work on a recognized holiday, they will receive holiday pay plus wages at their straight-time rate for the hours worked on the holiday.

In addition to the recognized holidays previously listed, eligible employees will receive one floating holiday in each anniversary year. To be eligible, employees must complete 90 calendar days of service in an eligible employment classification. These holidays must be scheduled at least one week in advance with the Operations Manager.

Paid time off for holidays will not be counted as hours worked for the purposes of determining overtime.

VACATIONS

Vacation days will accrue at a rate that depends upon the number of months of full-time employment under the following schedule:

Months Employed	Days Per Month Accrued
0 – 12	0.4166 (5 days per 12 months)
12 – 60	0.8333 (10 days per 12 months)
60 - 120	1.2500 (15 days per 12 months)
120 +	1.6666 (20 days per 12 months)

Vacation days available are calculated on a calendar basis and may be taken prior to being earned (after completing 12 months of employment). Vacation may be used in one-day increments.

To use less than three consecutive vacation days, an employee must request approval from his/her supervisor at least two weeks in advance. If the notice is shorter than two weeks, days taken are either personal days or are taken without pay.

A two-week notice is required to take three or more consecutive vacation days. If the notice is shorter than two weeks, days are taken without pay. Notice must be given to your supervisor.

Vacation time off is paid at the employee's base rate at the time of vacation. It does not include overtime or any special forms of compensation such as incentives, commissions, bonuses, or shift differentials.

Vacations are scheduled on a first-come, first-served basis. In the event of simultaneous requests, preference will be given to employees with seniority of service. Due to the volume of work immediately before and after January 1st, no employee may take more than three vacation days between December 15th and January 15th.

Any employee entitled to more than two weeks vacation normally may not use more than two weeks consecutively. No more than two weeks may be used in any consecutive three-month period.

Vacation days do not accrue from one year to the next and must be used during the current calendar year. Part-time employees do not earn vacation time.

Once employees reach their seventh month of employment, they can use vacation days before earned. In the event of voluntary or involuntary termination, any excess of days used over days earned will result in a deduction from their final pay.

PERSONAL (SICK) DAYS

<ENTER AGENCY NAME> provides paid sick leave benefits to all eligible employees for periods of temporary absence due to illnesses or injuries. Regular full-time employees are eligible.

Eligible employees will accrue sick leave benefits at the rate of 6 days per year (.50 of a day for every full month of service). Sick leave benefits are calculated on the basis of a "benefit year," the 12-month period that begins when the employee starts to earn sick leave benefits.

Employees can request use of paid sick leave after completing a waiting period of 180 calendar days from the date they become eligible to accrue sick leave benefits. Paid sick leave can be used in minimum increments of one day. Eligible employees may use sick leave benefits for an absence due to their own illness or injury or that of a family member who resides in the employee's household.
Employees who are unable to report to work due to illness or injury should notify their direct supervisor before the scheduled start of their workday if possible. The direct supervisor must also be contacted on each additional day of absence.

If an employee is absent for three or more consecutive days due to illness or injury, a physician's statement must be provided verifying the disability and its beginning and expected ending dates. Such verification may be requested for other sick leave absences as well and may be required as a condition to receiving sick leave benefits.

Before returning to work from a sick leave absence of three calendar days or more, an employee must provide a physician's verification that he or she may safely return to work.

Sick leave benefits will be calculated based on the employee's base pay rate at the time of absence and will not include any special forms of compensation, such as incentives, commissions, or bonuses.

As an additional condition of eligibility for sick leave benefits, an employee on an extended absence must apply for any other available compensation and benefits, such as workers' compensation. Sick leave benefits will be used to supplement any payments that an employee is eligible to receive from state disability insurance, or workers' compensation. The combination of any such disability payments and sick leave benefits cannot exceed the employee's normal weekly earnings.

Unused sick leave benefits will be allowed to accumulate until the employee has accrued a total of 9 days' worth of sick leave benefits. If the employee's benefits reach this maximum, further accrual of sick leave benefits will be suspended until the employee has reduced the balance below the limit.

Sick leave benefits are intended solely to provide income protection in the event of illness or injury, and may not be used for any other absence. Unused sick leave benefits will not be paid to employees while they are employed or upon termination of employment.

If an employee uses no sick leave benefits during an entire calendar year, he/she will be entitled to three (3) compensatory days off in the following calendar year.

REPORTING ABSENCES

Employees must notify the Office Manager by 9:00 a.m. on the day of the absence if they are unable to make it to work, due to illness or other reasons.

UNEXCUSED ABSENCES

Any absence from work not outlined above will be unexcused. During such periods, employees will not be paid wages.

MILITARY LEAVE

Employees needing time off for military service will be granted a leave of absence in accordance with the law governing military service and veterans' re-employment. Employees may request vacation pay from earned vacation benefits up to the total hours they have available to cover such a leave if they choose.

TIME OFF TO VOTE

<ENTER AGENCY NAME> encourages employees to fulfill their civic responsibilities by participating in elections. Generally, employees are able to find time to vote either before or after their regular work schedule. If employees are unable to vote in an election during their non-working hours, **<ENTER AGENCY NAME>** will comply with applicable laws in granting employees time off to vote.

Employees should request time off to vote from their supervisor at least two working days prior to the Election Day. Advance notice is required so that the necessary time off can be scheduled at the beginning or end of the work shift; whichever provides the least disruption to the normal work schedule.

BEREAVEMENT LEAVE

Employees who wish to take time off due to the death of an immediate family member should notify their supervisor immediately.

Up to two days of paid bereavement leave will be provided to regular full-time employees.

Bereavement pay is calculated based on the base pay rate at the time of absence and will not include any special forms of compensation, such as incentives, commissions, or bonuses.

Approval of bereavement leave will occur in the absence of unusual operating requirements. Employees may, with their supervisors' approval, use any available paid leave for additional time off as necessary.

<ENTER AGENCY NAME> defines "immediate family" as the employee's spouse, parent, child, or sibling; and the employee's spouse's parent, child, or sibling.

Attending the funeral of those other than "immediate family" defined above, with prior approval of immediate supervisor, will be allowed up to 3 hours' paid leave.

JURY DUTY

<ENTER AGENCY NAME> encourages employees to fulfill their civic responsibilities by serving jury duty when required. Employees who have completed a minimum of 90 calendar days of service in an eligible classification may request up to five days of paid jury duty leave over any two-year period. In addition, in compliance with federal law, exempt employees will be paid for any workweek in which the employee serves on jury duty and also performs any work.

Jury duty pay will be calculated on the employee's base pay rate times the number of hours the employee would otherwise have worked on the day of absence. Only regular full-time employees qualify for paid jury duty leave.

If employees are required to serve jury duty beyond the period of paid jury duty leave, they may use any available paid time off (for example, vacation benefits) or may request an unpaid jury duty leave of absence.

Employees must show the jury duty summons to their supervisor as soon as possible so that the supervisor may make arrangements to accommodate their absence. Eemployees are expected to report for work whenever the court schedule permits.

<ENTER AGENCY NAME> will continue to provide health insurance benefits for the full term of the jury duty absence.

Vacation, sick leave, and holiday benefits, will continue to accrue during unpaid jury duty leave.

WITNESS DUTY

<ENTER AGENCY NAME> encourages employees to appear in court for witness duty when subpoenaed to do so.

If employees have been subpoenaed or otherwise requested to testify as witnesses by **<ENTER AGENCY NAME>**, they will receive paid time off for the entire period of witness duty.

Employees will be granted unpaid time off to appear in court as a witness when requested by a party other than **<ENTER AGENCY NAME>**. Employees are free to use any available paid leave benefit (such as vacation leave) to receive compensation for the period of this absence.

The subpoena should be shown to the employee's supervisor immediately after it is received so that operating requirements can be adjusted, where necessary, to accommodate the employee's absence. The employee is expected to report for work whenever the court schedule permits.

GENERAL INFORMATION

ABSENTEE RECORDS

It is the Operations Manager's responsibility to record attendance for each employee on a daily basis. The attendance book also records personal and vacation days and recorded times that employees arrive to work late or left to go home early. If you wish to see your attendance record, please ask the Operations Manager to assist you.

ACCIDENTS

If employees incur work-related injury or illness, they must report it immediately to their Supervisor so they can be referred for necessary medical attention. Non-related illnesses or injuries also must be reported to your supervisor as soon as possible so that work coverage arrangements can be made.

AUTOMATION SYSTEM

The agency's automation system is essential to agency business operations. You are expected to maintain a complete and accurate database of client/policy information and accounting records for all clients and prospects assigned to you. You are expected to update and maintain the database for your clients and area of responsibility within agency standards.

You will be assigned a confidential password to use to enter the automation system. This password is to be used only by you. When you leave for lunch or are going to be away from your desk, you are expected to log off the automation system.

The automation system manager performs a back-up on the computer system each day. You are expected to sign off the system during the back up process.

BUSINESS TRAVEL

Any hotel and/or airfare in excess of $250 must be pre-approved by the President in writing. Failure to do so will result in the employee's being responsible for all expenses incurred on the trip.

FAMILY MEMBERS ON TRIPS

The employee must pay for any additional costs incurred due to family members traveling with the employee.

AIRFARE

If an employee is traveling during the week and there is a substantial airfare savings if employee would stay over Saturday night, **<ENTER AGENCY NAME>** will reimburse up to 50 percent of the difference in airfare cost to go towards hotel and car rental for that weekend. This must be pre-approved by the President.

FREQUENT FLYER PROGRAMS

Employees may earn the mileage for free trips and keep it for their personal use.

CHARITABLE CONTRIBUTIONS

The agency makes a variety of contributions to worthy causes. Refer all requests for agency sponsorship of local charitable organizations to the President. Priority will be given those organizations in which members of the staff and their families participate and to those organizations that are considered high visibility within the community.

COMPLAINT PROCEDURE

If an employee feels that any condition of employment affecting him/her creates a problem, the employee should use the following procedure to solve such problems without fear of reprisal.

1. The employee should discuss the matter with their supervisor.

2. Depending upon the circumstances, the supervisor should either respond immediately to the problem or study the situation and respond to the employee within three working days.

3. If the supervisor's response does not resolve the problem, the employee should discuss the matter with the supervisor's immediate supervisor.

4. If the problem directly involves the supervisor, the employee should discuss the problem with the next level supervisor.

If the concern involves possible unlawful harassment, discrimination or retaliation, the employee should follow the complaint procedure outlined in that policy.

CONFERENCE ROOM(S)

The conference room(s) are reserved through the receptionist, whowill need to know the date, time and approximate length of the meeting. Each department is responsible for its own "housekeeping" in the conference rooms as they are used.

CONFIDENTIALITY

Confidentiality should be maintained at all times about any client transaction or any client's business information. Also, as more fully set out in your individual confidentiality agreement, employees may not reveal either during or after their term of employment with **<ENTER AGENCY NAME>** any confidential information which was made available to them or to which they have gained access.

DESK AUDITS

To properly manage workflow and to ensure compliance with agency policies, management reserves the right to search any employee's desk at any time, regardless as to the employee's presence. You should not bring personal items into the agency that would be embarrassing if discovered by management.

DISABILITY ETIQUETTE

Don't let your uncertainty about how to act keep you from getting to know and conduct business with people with disabilities. Fear of the unknown and lack of knowledge about how to act can often lead to uneasiness when meeting a person with a disability. Just remember a person with a disability is a person. Treat him or her as you want to be treated.

DISCIPLINE

Occasionally management may conclude that an employee has failed to meet his or her obligations of attendance, behavior, or performance. In such situations, management will take the corrective measures it considers appropriate. Normally management will take into account the employee's overall performance, previous conduct, and length of service. The corrective measures which management may take include, but are not limited to, oral counseling, written documentation of the problem, probation, suspension without pay, and termination. If the matter is documented, the employee may be required to sign a copy of the documentation, which signature indicates only that the employee has received a copy of the documentation and not that the employee necessarily agrees with the documentation or the need for it.

DISHONESTY

The company will consider any dishonest act by an employee toward the company, another employee or towards a client of the company, regardless of the dollar amount, a criminal offense. Employment will be terminated. Criminal action may be taken.

DRESS STANDARDS

Employee appearance and dress is important in maintaining a professional image for **<ENTER AGENCY NAME>**. We frequently have visitors to our office and part of their perception of the agency is derived from the appearance of the employees. Employees help the agency assure a favorable impression by taking care in personal dress and grooming.

The desired image is a conservative and professional business environment. Part-time employees are expected to abide by the same rules as full time employees.

All employees are expected to report to work well-groomed and be conscious of good hygiene and attempt to maintain appropriate standards in this regard. Let common sense guide you in projecting this image.

Employee dress should be neat in appearance and in a manner consistent with a professional atmosphere, keeping in mind the desired impression to be made on clients, visitors and other employees. Appropriate undergarments must be worn.

Listed are some of the modes of dress that are unacceptable during normal working hours:

- Denim
- Casual shirts or T-shirts
- Sweat suits / Sweat shirts
- Blouses/shirts that have revealing necklines or midsections
- Tennis or athletic shoes
- Shorts

Violators of the dress code will be sent home immediately to change articles of clothing that do not conform to dress code standards. Repeated violations may result in disciplinary action. In each situation, the Operations Manager shall be the final arbiter of the suitability of attire.

DRUG-FREE WORKPLACE

It is the policy of **<ENTER AGENCY NAME>** to create a drug-free workplace. The use of alcohol or controlled substances is inconsistent with the behavior expected of employees, subjects all employees and visitors to our facilities to unacceptable safety risks, and undermines **<ENTER AGENCY NAME>** 's ability to operate effectively and efficiently.

Page 25 of 36

The unlawful manufacture, distribution, dispensation, possession, sale, or use of a controlled substance in the workplace, or while engaged in **<ENTER AGENCY NAME>** business off **<ENTER AGENCY NAME>**'s premises, is strictly prohibited. Such conduct is also prohibited during non-working time to the extent that in the opinion of **<ENTER AGENCY NAME>**, it impairs an employee's ability to perform on the job or threatens the reputation or integrity of **<ENTER AGENCY NAME>**.

Employees convicted of controlled substance related violations in the workplace, including pleas of nolo contendere (i.e., no contest), must inform **<ENTER AGENCY NAME>** within five days of such conviction or plea. Employees who violate any aspect of this policy may be subject to disciplinary action, up to and including termination. At its discretion, **<ENTER AGENCY NAME>** may require employees who violate this policy to successfully complete a drug abuse assistance or rehabilitation program as a condition of continued employment.

EDUCATIONAL ASSISTANCE

<ENTER AGENCY NAME> recognizes that the skills and knowledge of its employees are critical to the success of the organization. The educational assistance program encourages personal development through formal education so that employees can maintain and improve job-related skills or enhance their ability to compete for reasonably attainable jobs within **<ENTER AGENCY NAME>**.

<ENTER AGENCY NAME> will provide educational assistance to all eligible employees immediately upon assignment to an eligible employment classification. To maintain eligibility, employees must remain on the active payroll and be performing their job satisfactorily for the duration of each course.

In order to be eligible for educational assistance, individual courses or courses that are part of a degree, licensing, or certification program must be related to the employee's current job duties or a foreseeable future position in the organization. **<ENTER AGENCY NAME>** has the sole discretion to determine whether a course relates to an employee's current job duties or a foreseeable future position. Employees should contact the Operations Manager for more information about educational assistance.

While educational assistance is expected to enhance employees performance and professional abilities, **<ENTER AGENCY NAME>** cannot guarantee that participation in formal education will entitle the employee to automatic advancement, a different job assignment, or pay increases.

EMAIL & INTERNET USAGE

The agency's email system is for business use only. Employees should not utilize the email system for non-business usage, although occasional personal use is not prohibited if:
   a. It does not interfere with regular work,
   b. It does not generate a direct cost to the company,
   c. It does not have the appearance of being an official communication of the company (i.e., users should not use the Company address in personal communications), and
   d. It is not deemed to be improper, including use that:
   (i) Is disruptive or offensive to others, including, but not limited to, the transmission of chain letters or hate mail;

(ii) Can be construed as harassment or disparagement of others, including sexually explicit messages, or ethnic or racial slurs;

(iii) Is illegal or unethical, or misrepresents the employee or the company;

(iv) Constitutes the transmission of confidential information to unauthorized persons; or

(v) Consists of viewing objectionable, degrading, or inappropriate websites.

Management reserves the right to read all internal as well as external (both incoming and outgoing) emails.

Your job may require you to access the internet. Usage of the internet is restricted to business-related sites. Management will monitor internet usage for inappropriate use.

EMERGENCY CLOSINGS

At times, emergencies such as severe weather, fires, power failures, or earthquakes, may disrupt company operations. In extreme cases, these circumstances may require the closing of a work facility. Never place yourself in danger in an attempt to come into the office when it has been closed due to emergency conditions.

EMPLOYEE LOANS

<ENTER AGENCY NAME> does not provide Employee Loans.

EMPLOYEE PERSONNEL RECORDS

There is only one official personnel file for each employee of the company. The Operations Manager maintains this file.

It is your responsibility to keep your personnel records up to date. Inform the Operations Manager immediately if you have a change in your name, address, marital status, beneficiaries to be named on insurance policies or retirement plans, persons to be notified in event of an emergency, or military status (if applicable).

It is also important that the agency be notified when you receive any special awards, recognition or certifications. This information is used when developing promotional pieces for the agency and for developing the biographical sketch that is used in insurance proposals where you are involved.

Personnel files are the property of **<ENTER AGENCY NAME>**, and access to the information they contain is restricted. Generally, only supervisors and management personnel of **<ENTER AGENCY NAME>** who have a legitimate reason to review information in a file are allowed to do so.

Employees who wish to review their own file should contact the Operations Manager. With reasonable advance notice, current employees may review their own personnel files in **<ENTER AGENCY NAME>**'s offices and in the presence of an individual appointed by **<ENTER AGENCY NAME>** to maintain the files.

Page 27 of 36

EMPLOYEE SOLICITATIONS

In an effort to assure a productive and harmonious work environment, persons not employed by **<ENTER AGENCY NAME>** may not solicit or distribute literature in the workplace at any time for any purpose.

<ENTER AGENCY NAME> recognizes that employees may have interests in events and organizations outside the workplace. However, employees may not solicit or distribute literature concerning these activities during working time. (Working time does not include lunch periods, work breaks, or any other periods in which employees are not on duty.)

Examples of impermissible forms of solicitation include:

The collection of money, goods, or gifts for political groups
The circulation of petitions
The distribution of literature not approved by the employer
The solicitation of memberships, fees, or dues

EMPLOYEE SUGGESTION PROGRAM

Employees are encouraged to provide the company with written suggestions and comments about company policies and programs.

EXPENSE REPORT POLICY

Expense reports must be submitted to the Chief Financial Officer no later than 11:30 a.m. on the 10th day of the month unless otherwise notified by the accounting department. Reimbursement checks will be issued with the mid-month payroll checks.

SPOUSES AND BUSINESS DINNERS

<ENTER AGENCY NAME> will reimburse 50 percent of a spouse's meal if the meal is business-related and is pre-approved by the President.

EVENT TICKETS

Reimbursement for these tickets must be pre-approved by the President.

HARASSMENT POLICY

<ENTER AGENCY NAME> is committed to the principle that all employees have the right to work in an environment free of discrimination and any form of harassment based on race, color, religion, age, sex, national origin, disability, sexual orientation or marital status.

As used in this policy statement, the term "harassment" shall include, but not be limited to, the following:

1. Unwelcome or unwanted advances, including sexual advances. This means patting, pinching, brushing up against, hugging, cornering, kissing, fondling, or any other similar physical contact considered unacceptable by the other individual.

2. Requests or demands for favors, including sexual favors. This includes subtle or blatant expectations, pressures or requests for any type of favor, including a sexual favor, accompanied by an implied or stated promise of preferential treatment or negative consequences concerning one's employment status.

3. Verbal abuse or kidding that is oriented toward a prohibited form of harassment, including that which is sexually oriented and considered unacceptable by another individual. This includes, for example, commenting about an individual's national origin, race, body or appearance where such comments go beyond mere courtesy; telling "dirty jokes" or racial ethnic jokes that are unwanted and considered offensive by others; or any tasteless sexually, ethnically, or racially oriented comments, innuendoes, or actions that offend others.

4. Engaging in any type of sexually oriented conduct or other form of harassment that would unreasonably interfere with another's work performance. This includes extending unwanted sexual attentions to someone that reduces that person's productivity or time available to work at assigned tasks.

5. Creating a work environment that is intimidating, hostile, abusive, or offensive because of unwelcome or unwanted conversations, suggestions, requests, demands, physical contacts or attentions, whether sexually oriented or otherwise related to some other form of harassment.

Each member of management is responsible for creating an atmosphere free of discrimination and harassment, sexual or otherwise. Further, employees are responsible for respecting the rights of their coworkers.

If you experience any job-related harassment based on your sex, race, national origin, disability, or another factor, or believe that you have been treated in an unlawful, discriminatory manner, promptly report the incident to your supervisor, who will investigate the matter and take appropriate action, including reporting it to the director of human resources. If you believe it would be inappropriate to discuss the matter with your supervisor, you may bypass your supervisor and report it directly to the head of your department or to the Operations Manager, who will undertake an investigation. Your complaint will be kept confidential to the maximum extent possible.

If **<ENTER AGENCY NAME>** determines that an employee is guilty of harassing another individual, appropriate disciplinary action will be taken against the offending employee, up to and including termination of employment.

<ENTER AGENCY NAME> prohibits any form of retaliation against any employee for filing a bona fide complaint under this policy or for assisting in a complaint investigation. However, if, after investigating any complaint of harassment or unlawful discrimination, **<ENTER AGENCY NAME>** determines that the complaint is not bona fide or that an employee has provided false information regarding the complaint, disciplinary action may be taken against the individual who filed the complaint or who gave the false information.

HEALTH AND SAFETY

All personnel have the responsibility to be aware of the importance of taking proper safety precautions. Such efforts include but are not limited to:

1. Removing or covering telephone or other electrical cords in aisles or walkways to prevent injury.

2. Storing equipment, supply cartons, and supplies in areas not subject to employee traffic.

3. Using proper equipment to move heavy objects (furniture, files and equipment).

The Occupational Safety and Health Act defines health and safety standards for working conditions, provides for inspections, and requires that employees follow special internal reporting procedures and maintain detailed records of employee occupation injury or illness. Be sure to report any occupational injury or illness to your manager immediately.

LEAVES OF ABSENCE

A leave of absence without pay will be granted to an employee for a period of up to twelve weeks. The leave of absence is available to full-time regular employees. The leave may be taken upon the birth of the employee's child; upon placement of a child with the employee for adoption; when the employee is needed to care for a child, spouse, or parent who has a serious health condition; or when the employee is unable to perform the duties of his or her position because of a serious health condition.

<ENTER AGENCY NAME> will require medical certification to support a claim for leave for the employee's own serious health condition or to care for a seriously ill child, spouse, or parent. In its discretion, **<ENTER AGENCY NAME>** may require a second medical opinion at its own expense.

To be eligible for leave under this policy an employee must have been employed full time for at least twelve consecutive months preceding the commencement of the leave.

When the need for leave is foreseeable, such as the birth or adoption of a child, or planned medical treatment, the employee must provide reasonable prior notice, and make efforts to schedule leave so as not to disrupt **<ENTER AGENCY NAME>** operations. When the need for leave is unforeseeable, the employee should give notice to **<ENTER AGENCY NAME>** as soon as practical. In cases of illness, the employee will be required to report periodically on his or her leave status and intention to return to work.

LICENSING

Employees involved in handling insurance placement or contact with clients for insurance reasons must maintain the proper insurance license. The agency will pay for the insurance license fee.

LIFE-THREATENING ILLNESSES IN THE WORKPLACE

Employees with life-threatening illnesses, such as cancer, heart disease, or AIDS, often wish to continue their normal pursuits, including work, to the extent allowed by their condition. **<ENTER AGENCY NAME>** supports these endeavors as long as employees are able to meet acceptable performance standards.

Managing Human Resources in an Insurance Agency **151**

Medical information on individual employees is treated confidentially. **<ENTER AGENCY NAME>** will take reasonable precautions to protect such information from inappropriate disclosure. Managers and other employees have a responsibility to respect and maintain the confidentiality of employee medical information. Anyone inappropriately disclosing such information is subject to disciplinary action, up to and including termination of employment.

Employees with questions or concerns about life-threatening illnesses are encouraged to contact the Operations Manager or **<ENTER AGENCY NAME>**'s Employee Assistance Program for information and referral to appropriate services and resources.

MAIL

INCOMING MAIL

Incoming mail will be opened, date stamped, and distributed promptly. All mail, even mail marked Personal & Confidential will be opened by the mail clerk.

No personal mail should be received at the office. This includes personal magazine subscriptions and catalogs.

OUTGOING MAIL

Outgoing mail must meet agency standards for professional appearance and content. Outgoing mail may be audited by management to assure quality control.

The mail clerk sorts outgoing U.S. mail at 4:00 PM each day. The mailroom should be notified of all large mailings in advance.

Only the mail clerk is authorized to operate the mailing machine. No personal mail will be run through the postage machine.

Pre-approval from the Office Manager or the Department Manager is necessary for all courier services or overnight delivery.

MANAGEMENT RIGHTS

Management reserves the right to make changes in its benefits, policies, procedures and operations as it may deem necessary without prior notice.

NON SMOKING POLICY

The agency will comply with all applicable federal, state and local regulations regarding smoking in the work place. Smoking is prohibited inside all agency facilities and applies to employees, clients, and visitors while on the premises. The agency does not discriminate against individuals who smoke during non-work time.

Page 31 of 36

OFFICE APPEARANCE

We are proud of our office; it is neatly organized and an attractive place to work. In order to maintain this environment, you are asked to contribute to the general maintenance of your work area and the entire office.

1. Please keep your desk neatly organized.
2. Keep only necessary materials pertaining to your job requirements on your desk.
3. Keep file folders vertically filed on your desk throughout the day.
4. Please keep your machines covered at night to protect them from dust.
5. Copier should be neat and clean at all times.
6. Your work area must be clean. Please use a dust cloth regularly for your entire work area, including file cabinets, bookcases, etc. located near you.
7. When leaving at night, clear your entire work area of all paperwork and properly store everything.
8. The conference room must be left as you found it.

OFFICE CONDUCT

We believe a friendly team effort is the best way to be successful. As we grow, it is essential that we maintain friendliness toward each other. One way to help assure this is to use first names. However, please use discretion when addressing a client or company representative. If no indication is given, use a Mr. or Ms. title when addressing external contacts.

Visiting and conversing at length with co-workers should pertain only to business matters. Minimize personal visits during work hours.

Courtesy to fellow employees is mandatory, office visitors, and people who call the office.

OFFICE MEETINGS

Meetings will be held periodically at **<ENTER AGENCY NAME>** to discuss new procedures or problems. Employees are encouraged to contribute to discussions in these office meetings; suggestions and criticisms about our procedures, policies, and systems are always welcome.

Employees may be required to attend office meetings prior to or after working hours on occasion. Any difficulty in attending such meetings should be discussed with your immediate supervisor in advance.

OFFICE SUPPLIES

The Office Manager has full responsibility for ordering supplies and keeping a full inventory. When supplies are delivered to the office, let the Office Manager know that the supplies have arrived. Please consult with the Office Manager about ordering supplies; do not order them yourself.

OPEN DOOR POLICY

Our door is always open to you. If you have a problem you need to discuss with us, please discuss this matter first with your supervisor. If the matter remains unresolved, we maintain an "open door" policy for you to discuss your problem with the management.

OUTSIDE EMPLOYMENT

An employee may hold a job with another organization as long as he or she satisfactorily performs his or her job responsibilities with **<ENTER AGENCY NAME>**. All employees will be judged by the same performance standards and will be subject to **<ENTER AGENCY NAME>**'s scheduling demands, regardless of any existing outside work requirements.

If **<ENTER AGENCY NAME>** determines that an employee's outside work interferes with performance or the ability to meet the requirements of **<ENTER AGENCY NAME>** as they are modified from time to time, the employee may be asked to terminate the outside employment if he or she wishes to remain with **<ENTER AGENCY NAME>**.

Outside employment will present a conflict of interest if it has an adverse impact on **<ENTER AGENCY NAME>**.

PERSONAL TELEPHONE USAGE

<ENTER AGENCY NAME> realizes that occasionally it will be necessary for employees to receive important personal telephone calls during working hours. Although these telephone calls are not prohibited, they should be limited to a maximum of five minutes and should be held to a minimum.

PETTY CASH

Requests for petty cash are to be made to the Accounting Manager. When using petty cash, you must sign a receipt for our records.

RECORDS RETENTION

No record of any kind may be destroyed without prior approval of management.

RESPONSIBILITY FOR DEPOSITS

Some employees are responsible for receiving cash, checks, and money orders from clients. These funds must be properly receipted and forwarded to the accounting department. In the event that an employee's deposit is short, the shortfall will be deducted from the employee's paycheck.

SECURITY INSPECTIONS

<ENTER AGENCY NAME> wishes to maintain a work environment that is free of illegal drugs, alcohol, firearms, explosives, or other improper materials. To this end, **<ENTER AGENCY NAME>** prohibits the possession, transfer, sale, or use of such materials on its premises. **<ENTER AGENCY NAME>** requires the cooperation of all employees in administering this policy.

Desks, lockers, and other storage devices may be provided for the convenience of employees but remains the sole property of **<ENTER AGENCY NAME>**. Accordingly, they, as well as any articles found within them, can be inspected by any agent or representative of **<ENTER AGENCY NAME>** at any time, either with or without prior notice or the presense of the employee.

<ENTER AGENCY NAME> likewise wishes to discourage theft or unauthorized possession of the property of employees, **<ENTER AGENCY NAME>**, visitors, and customers. To facilitate enforcement of this policy, **<ENTER AGENCY NAME>** or its representative may inspect not only desks and lockers but also persons entering and/or leaving the premises and any packages or other belongings. Any employee who wishes to avoid inspection of any articles or materials should not bring such items onto **<ENTER AGENCY NAME>**'s premises.

SAFEGUARDING COMPANY & PERSONAL PROPERTY

Employees are expected to take all precautions necessary to assure that company equipment and other property is not lost, damaged or stolen.

<ENTER AGENCY NAME> assumes no responsibility for the recovery or replacement of personal property damaged, lost, or stolen. All personal items should be safeguarded. Locking valuable items in a desk or file cabinet can help prevent theft. However, the corporation's officers will have 24-hour access to all drawers and files.

TELEPHONE ETIQUETTE

Good telephone habits demonstrate that **<ENTER AGENCY NAME>** is efficient and friendly as well as helpful and considerate. The following guide is a suggested basis for good telephone courtesy:

1. Answer promptly (within three rings), accurately, and carefully.

2. Identify yourself by name and department.

3. Return all calls before the end of the business day.

4. Voicemail messages should state that coverage cannot be bound via the voicemail system.

5. Transfer calls promptly and tactfully.

6. Hang up quietly, after the other party has hung up.

WORKER'S COMPENSATION

<ENTER AGENCY NAME> carries workers compensation insurance to protect all **<ENTER AGENCY NAME>** employees in case of accident and injury while at work. If an employee is injured while at work, report the incident immediately to the employee's Supervisor. An injured employee may be required to be medically examined and/or treated.

In the event of an injury, Incident Report Forms are to be completed immediately, or as soon as practicable, by the employee with the assistance of their Supervisor, and forwarded to the insurance carrier.

WORKING TOGETHER

We prefer to deal with people directly rather than through a third party. We operate on the simple, basic idea that if we treat all employees fairly and promote a positive feeling for providing the highest quality products and services to our clients, **<ENTER AGENCY NAME>** will be the best possible place for everyone to work. We know that no workplace is free from day to day problems. Nevertheless, we believe that we can best work out our problems among ourselves. We encourage you to bring your problems to your supervisor or anyone in administration you feel can help you. We promise to listen and give you a straightforward answer.

WORKPLACE SEARCHES

To safeguard the property of our employees, our clients, and **<ENTER AGENCY NAME>**, and to help maintain a smooth flow of work, **<ENTER AGENCY NAME>** reserves the right to search any employee's office, desk, files, or any other area or article on our premises. In this connection, it should be noted that all offices, desks, files, and so forth, are the property of **<ENTER AGENCY NAME>**, and are issued for the use of employees only during their employment with **<ENTER AGENCY NAME>**. Inspections may be conducted at any time at the discretion of **<ENTER AGENCY NAME>** management.

Employees working on, or entering or leaving the premises, who refuse to cooperate in an inspection, as well as employees who after the inspection are believed to be in possession of stolen property or illegal drugs, will be sent immediately to the human resources department and will be subject to disciplinary action up to and including discharge if on investigation they are found to be in violation of **<ENTER AGENCY NAME>**'s security procedures or any other **<ENTER AGENCY NAME>** rules and regulations.

EMPLOYEE MANUAL ACKNOWLEDGMENT

Acknowledgment:

I acknowledge that I have received a printed copy of the **<ENTER AGENCY NAME>** Employee Manual. I acknowledge that I am expected to know and be familiar with the contents and that I have read the manual and will abide by its contents. I further acknowledge that I have been given the opportunity to ask any questions I might have regarding the contents.

I understand:

- That this manual can be updated at any time, for any reason.

- That this is an employee manual rather than an express or implied contract.

- That I am an employee at will of **<ENTER AGENCY NAME>** and that I may resign or be terminated at any time.

- That this manual is the property of **<ENTER AGENCY NAME>**.

_____   _____

Employee Signature   Date

_____   _____

Name (please print)   Date

Page 36 of 36

Section 5: Procedures Manual
Developing a Procedures Manual

The more you can do to automate and streamline the agency's processes, the lower the expense load. A procedures manual will help make the processes consistent.

However, most agencies do not have a procedures manual. Some of the reasons for this are:

1. Don't have the time to put one together.

2. Don't know how to start.

3. Afraid staff will not follow it.

4. Don't have the determination to enforce it.

If you are going to take the time to create a procedures manual, you must have a strong management commitment to enforce it and keep it up to date. If you don't have this determination, don't waste your time, money, and effort creating one.

A procedures or workflow manual is a "how to" guide that focuses on the flow of work and focuses on your systems and clients. It should focus on the systems and procedures within an agency that are used to accomplish specific functions. . To keep pace with internal and external changes, someone in the agency will need to review and update the manual regularly.

But, do you really need a workflow manual? Probably so. The development of one should help you focus on staff stratification. Staff stratification is when you transfer work in an agency to the lowest cost level, i.e., the lowest paid employee who is capable of handling the work in a satisfactory manner.

For instance, while an agency thinks it needs to hire an additional producer to increase production, it may in fact need more clerical help. Hiring clerical help for the CSRs can free up the CSRs' time, which, in turn,, which, in turn, frees up the CSRs to take some of the workload off the producers. With additional time, the existing producers can generate new accounts.

Analyzing who does what (job descriptions), and how the work flows in an agency (procedures manual), can help the agency identify what work can be transferred to lower paid employees.

Items such as auto ID cards and certificates of insurance can and should be delegated to those employees with the least experience. The more complex tasks, as well as critical accounts, should remain with more experienced employees.

What are the characteristics of a good procedures manual? It should:

1. Be in writing.

2. Be a set of procedures used to accomplish a specific task.

3. Be structured so that it minimizes the number of times an item is handled during each step of the process.

4. Minimize any backlog.

5. Be used as a training tool for new employees.

6. Be used by all staff as a reference tool and single source of information.

7. Help minimize E&O exposures.

8. Support your defense in the event of an E&O claim.

By having everyone in the agency follow the same system:

1. Someone else in can take over where the first person left off.

2. Anyone in the agency can understand the status of an account.

3. Managers can verify that all employees are performing the functions properly.

4. Efficiency and productivity will be increased.

In addition to improving efficiency and thus increasing agency value, a good procedures manual should help reduce errors and omissions exposures. Unless you have outlined specific steps to complete a given task, it is quite possible that employees could miss, skip, or even ignore certain tasks, which can result in errors and omissions. While developing, instituting, and enforcing standards will not eliminate your E&O exposures, those steps can certainly reduce them.

To develop a procedures manual, an agency must break down each process into its component tasks. The problem, as stated earlier, is that most agencies don't want to take the time to develop a manual, and the temptation is to just "buy one off the shelf." However, this is not a good idea since the processes should be tailored to the unique needs of your agency.

Some items you need to consider when developing a procedures manual are:

Level of Automation – Is your agency automated or manual? If you are manual, something like rating a risk will include steps such as updating the rate sheets or calling the carrier for a quote. And, if you want comparative quotes, you will need to contact multiple carriers. This may entail faxing or mailing information to the carrier and then pending for follow-up.

However, if you are automated and have a comparative rater, you can input the information one time and have multiple quotes at your fingertips. Think about it. You've eliminated the need for calling, faxing, or mailing documents to multiple carriers, and the need for pending for follow-up. How much time did you save? It adds up. Additionally, quicker response to your client's requests should improve retention. If it is a prospect, fast responsiveness is impressive.

How you do Business with Your Carriers – Do you utilize the upload and/or download capabilities of your carriers? If you don't, you again need to fax, mail, or email information and pend for follow-up. When the documents come back, you need to spend time verifying you received what you requested. If you have carrier upload / download, once the data is uploaded you only need to verify what is downloaded or look at any exception report the system provides.

Some carriers have their own unique way of doing things, such as handling claims or quoting business. Has a carrier given you binding authority or claims settling authority? If so, you will need to develop procedures on a carrier-by-carrier basis. But before you do that, you should determine how much additional time and effort goes into this alternate process. Then look at the commissions generated by this carrier and decide if it is worth having that carrier in your agency.

Carrier Provided Services – What services does the carrier service center provide? If your carriers handle all the servicing issues, this will reduce your servicing procedures, but your call transfer process becomes more important.

Does you carrier round out accounts? If so, how do you handle situations where a client's policies are spread among two or more carriers? And with a carrier servicing your accounts, what changes to your procedures will need to be made so that the client feels you are needed?

Billing – If your agency does agency billing, what are the collection procedures? Who has the authority to cancel a client for non-pay? When do you cancel a client for non-payment? If you are on a direct bill basis, the collection procedures aren't as important, but how do you record the commission received from those carriers.

Filing Methods – Are you filling manually, transactionally, or are you scanning? With manual filing, you need to decide who sets up new files and files away the documents, and the order the documents are to appear in the file. Transactional filing reduces filing time , but who is responsible for retrieving documents? And what about dead files? With scanning, you do not retain the paper after it is scanned, so you never need to destroy "old" files. With manual filing, you need to decide at what point you can discard old documents, which documents, and what the process is to destroy them.

As you can see, the above five factors can greatly affect the procedures you institute in your agency, and thus the content of the procedures manual. The issue then arises as to the format.

One key factor is to refer to positions in an agency, not to people. For example: if the manual says, "Mary answers incoming calls in three rings" it becomes obsolete if Mary leaves the agency or transfers to another position. If you state that the "Receptionist" answers the telephone in three rings, it doesn't matter who is in that position, Mary, Sue, or Joe.

Agencies that automated usually have activity codes. When developing a procedure, determine what activity code (if any) should be used for each step in a task. Failure to do so could result in your six CSRs using six different codes in the same situation. Remember, you want everyone to be able to look at a client's record and immediately understand the status of the account. You cannot do that if different people are using different activity codes.

Finally, from an efficiency standpoint and an E&O standpoint, the agency should use form letters when appropriate. If you have a standard form letter for a particular step in a process, refer to that letter in your manual.

To make your procedures manual easy to understand, update, and maintain, consider setting it up in table format in your word processing system. A good format would be:

Step	Person Responsible	Activity Code	Form Letter
1.			
2.			
3.			

A critical issue that needs to be address is what level of detail you want in your procedures manual. Too much detail makes it obsolete more quickly. Not enough detail can result in too many questions from employees. Ideally, the manual should address the "flow" of work in the agency and touch on the major steps that "must" be executed.

Most procedures manuals should be split into sections, such as:

1. General and Administrative

2. Accounting

3. Life & Benefits

4. Commercial Lines

5. Personal Lines

By doing this, you don't need to provide everyone in the agency with a complete manual. It's not necessary for a Personal Lines CSR to be familiar with the Life and Benefits procedures, but she needs to be an expert and fully understand the personal lines procedures. You don't want an OBT (On Board Terrorist). These are the employees who follow the Frank Sinatra process: "I'll Do It My Way."

Employees who do it their own way cause the agency potential E&O exposures and can cost the agency in terms of productivity and efficiency. These employees need to be retrained to follow the rules. If they don't, get rid of them.

As stated previously, you cannot buy an "off the shelf" procedures manual; it needs to be tailored to your agency. However, if you are going to develop a manual for your agency, it's good to have one to review and adapt it to suit your needs.

Due to the factors previously outlined in this section, procedures can, will, and should vary from agency to agency. The following sample procedures were developed for an automated agency that was using transactional filing. It has been sanitized to eliminate references to unique carrier requirements, the agency's activity codes, and references to agency form letters.

There is no guarantee that these procedures are complete or accurate or that they will reduce E&O exposures. They are merely offered here as a starting point for you to develop a procedures manual for your agency. Use them at your own risk.

Exhibit: Procedures Manual

PROCEDURES MANUAL: TABLE OF CONTENTS

GENERAL & ADMINISTRATIVE PROCEDURES

ACCOUNTING PROCEDURES

LIFE & HEALTH PROCEDURES

COMMERCIAL LINES PROCEDURES

PERSONAL LINES PROCEDURES

GENERAL & ADMINISTRATIVE PROCEDURES

SETTING UP CARRIER FILES

Step	Person Responsible	Activity Code	Form Letter
1. Contract is reviewed and signed.	President		
2. Type up label and set up folder for new carriers.	Administrative Assistant		
3. Insert papers into appropriate file.	Administrative Assistant		

SUPPLY ORDERING

Step	Person Responsible	Activity Code	Form Letter
1. When anyone who takes the next to last item must indicate shortage on supply sheet and give notification to appropriate individual.	Employee taking item		
2. Uncommon item requests must be submitted on form to appropriate individual by Friday for purchase the following Tuesday.	Employee requesting item		
3. Uncommon item requests given to appropriate individual for approval.	File Clerk		
4. Approves or disapproves requests & returns to appropriate individual.	Office Manager		
5. Inventory supplies on Monday.	File Clerk		
6. Order supplies on Tuesday with expected delivery on Wednesday.	File Clerk		
7. When supplies arrive, checks the invoice and call vendor about any problems or discrepancies.	File Clerk		
8. Place items in proper supply area.	File Clerk		

Page 3 of 28

INCOMING MAIL

Step	Person Responsible	Activity Code	Form Letter
1. As soon as mail arrives it is worked on immediately.	File Clerk		
2. ALL MAIL, both postal service and inter-office (unless it specifically says "Personal & Confidential") is opened.	File Clerk		
3. Opened mail is date stamped on front page and envelope is stapled to documents. Unopened Personal & Confidential mail is date stamped on envelope	File Clerk		
4. Personal Lines mail is distributed to the CSR responsible (as indicated on automation system) for that account.	File Clerk		
5. Commercial Lines mail is distributed to the CSR responsible (as indicated on automation system) for that account.	File Clerk		
6. All incoming checks (both commission and policy payments) are sent to accounting manager, unless the policy payments are specifically addressed to a CSR or Producer, in which case they should be given to that CSR or Producer.	File Clerk		
7. Mail is placed in each employees "in-box."	File Clerk		
8. Mail returned by US Post Office is opened by file clerk and sent to originator. Originator is responsible for resending and correcting address in automation system.	Mail originator		

OUTGOING MAIL

Step	Person Responsible	Activity Code	Form Letter
Mail not time sensitive (Bulk mailings)			
1. Each employee is responsible for preparing his or her own mail, excluding postage.	All employees		
2. Deliver mail to regular out-going mail tray located at file clerk's station by 4:30pm each day for mailing that day.	All employees		
3. Add postage, bundle mail.	File Clerk		
4. Place bundles into box for mail pickup by 4:45pm for pickup the same day.	File Clerk		
Time sensitive mail (Overnight, Priority, etc.)			
1. Each employee is responsible for preparing his or her own mail, excluding postage.	All employees		
2. Deliver mail to meter out-going mail tray located at file clerk's station by 4:30pm each day for mailing that day.	All employees		
3. Run mail through postage meter and puts in U.S. mailbox by 5pm for pickup that day.	File Clerk		

INCOMING TELEPHONE CALLS

Step	Person Responsible	Activity Code	Form Letter
1. Calls coming into the switchboard are answered within three rings in a professional and courteous manner.	Receptionist		
2. Call is routed to the most appropriate department or person in the most efficient manner possible. This would include looking up clients in automation system and asking the proper questions	Receptionist		
3. If line is not busy, call is answered by employee within three rings in a professional and courteous manner. Employee must answer phone unless a client is in their office.	Employee		
4. If line is busy or not picked up, call goes to voice mail. All voice mail messages are to be returned within 24 hours of receipt.	Employee		

EMAIL

Step	Person Responsible	Activity Code	Form Letter
1. Every morning by 9:00 a.m. Common Email is retrieved.	Receptionist		
2. Distribute Email to the appropriate person(s).	Receptionist		
3. Personally addressed email must be read the same day it is received.			

FAXES

Step	Person Responsible	Activity Code	Form Letter
Outgoing			
1. Outgoing faxes are given to appropriate individual.	Fax originator		
2. Send outgoing fax.	File Clerk		
3. Attach confirmation to document and route back to originator.	File Clerk		
4. Machine prints out outgoing fax log at end of day. Put it in binder.	File Clerk		
Incoming faxes			
1. Incoming fax is logged in on form as to from whom, to whom, date, # of pages.	File Clerk		
2. Verify date on incoming fax is accurate. If not accurate, date stamp with mail "Received" date stamp.			
3. Route fax to destination.	File Clerk		

CLOSE DAY REPORTS

Step	Person Responsible	Activity Code	Form Letter
1. Close day runs automatically at 7:00pm each evening.	Automated		
2. Printed reports are retrieved and distributed to the appropriate person the next morning by 9:00am.	Automation Manager		

LICENSING

Step	Person Responsible	Activity Code	Form Letter
New Licenses for the Agency			
1. Management requests to start application process.	Management		
2. Order application from state & pends for 30 days.	Office Manager		
3. Complete application with 3 days of arrival.	Office Manager		
4. File application with check.	Office Manager		
5. Pend for 60 days to check status.	Office Manager		
Renewing Licenses For the Agency			
1. Receive renewal application.	Office Manager		
2. Complete it within 3 days of receipt.	Office Manager		
3. File it with check.	Office Manager		
4. If lapse notice arrives, investigate.	Office Manager		
Licensing for New Employees			
1. During interview process, agent is required to provide copy of all licenses.	Interviewer		
2. Contact the insurance department to inquire about complaints and to verify license is still active.	Office Manager		
3. Report findings back to management. (An offer for employment cannot be extended until licensing status is verified.)	Office Manager		

Page 6 of 28

LICENSING (Continued)

Step	Person Responsible	Activity Code	Form Letter
Existing Agent – New state			
1. All agents should be licensed in all states where business is actively marketed by the agency.	Office Manager		
2. Track licensing via database program.	Office Manager		
3. Give applications to agents to complete.	Office Manager		
4. Complete application within 7 days and return.	Agent		
5. Issue check & mail. Pend for 60-day follow-up.	Office Manager		
Existing Agent – Renewal			
1. Give application to agent to complete.	Office Manager		
2. Agent completes and returns within 7 days.	Agent		
3. Issue check & mail. Pend for 60-day follow-up.	Office Manager		
Credit Life Licensing			
1. Complete application within 7 days of receipt.	Agent		
2. Send transmittal sheet, check and application to carrier. Pend for 60-day follow-up.	Office Manager		
3. Carrier sends application & money to the state.	Carrier		
4. Add to employee list.	Office Manager		
5. Receive terminating employee list from HR dept.	Office Manager		
6. Send termination form to state along with check within 30 days of termination.	Office Manager		
7. Pend for 60 days for verification from state.	Office Manager		

EDUCATION & TRAINING

Step	Person Responsible	Activity Code	Form Letter
1. Track continuing education requirements.	Office Manager		
2. Circulate fliers or marketing information on available CE classes.	Office Manager		
3. Recommend classes for employees to take.	Office Manager		
4. Investigate bringing classes in house for cost effectiveness.	Office Manager		
5. Employees are required to take certification tests if offered (CIC, CPCU).	Office Manager		
6. Certification classes are reimbursed 75% upon registration and 25% upon successful completion.	Office Manager		
7. Licensed employees are given a continuing education status update semi-annually in May and November.	Office Manager		

ACCOUNTING PROCEDURES

CLIENT STATEMENTS & INVOICES

Step	Person Responsible	Activity Code	Form Letter
Debit Balances			
1. Run debit balance client statements on the 20th of the month.	Accountant		
2. If CSR and/or Producer doesn't want a client statement to be mailed, CSR must inform appropriate individual by the 19th of the month and give a valid reason.	CSR		
3. Put client statements in mail (not given to CSR). Include return envelope.	Accountant		
Credit Balances			
1. Investigate credit balance clients with a credit balance aged over 90 days.	Accountant		
2. If client is paid up and no future installments are scheduled, issue a refund check.	Accountant		
3. Refund check is mailed to client along with a form letter explaining what the check is for.	CSR		
Memo Invoices			
1. Under no circumstances should a Memo billing be done on Direct Bill accounts, instead, a form letter should be sent to client indicating they should expect an invoice from the carrier.	CL CSR		

ACCOUNTS PAYABLE (CARRIERS)

Step	Person Responsible	Activity Code	Form Letter
1. Verify carrier detail matches the GL total. If not in balance, correct discrepancies.	Accountant		
2. Reconcile carrier statements to automation system & only pay carrier on collected items.	Accountant		
3. If item is on statement but not in automation system, copy of carrier statement is sent to CSR handling account.	Accountant		
4. CSR corrects & returns copy of statement within five working days.	CSR		
5. Indicate on statement why items are not being paid.	Accountant		
6. Check is cut to carrier on collected items.	Accountant		
7. Check & copy of statement is mailed to carrier so it is received on a timely basis.	Accountant		
8. Copy of the check, carrier statement & automation system printout is filed by carrier.	Accountant		
9. Investigate all old items (90+ days) that have not appeared on a Carrier statement.	Accountant		

Page 9 of 28

ACCOUNTS PAYABLE (VENDORS)

Step	Person Responsible	Activity Code	Form Letter
1. All bills are given to appropriate individual.	Accountant		
2. Bills are reconciled to shipping order if there is one.	Accountant		
3. Unusual bills are investigated.	Accountant		
4. Regular bills – checks are cut & attached to invoice. Unusual bills are approved first, before checks are cut.	Accountant		
5. Checks are submitted for two signatures. (Employees cannot sign their own expense reports.)	President & other authorized signer		
6. Individual expense reports must first be approved by employee's manager before being sent to accounting.	Appropriate Manager		
7. Make copies of checks & attach copies to invoice, which is then filed by GL Account #.	Accountant		
8. Mail/distribute checks prior to due date or within five days of receipt, whichever is later.	Accountant		

EXPENSE REPORTS

Step	Person Responsible	Activity Code	Form Letter
1. Employee completes expense report by the 20th of the month. Must attach original receipts.	Employee		
2. Employee gives report to manager for approval.	Employee		
3. Manager amends expense report as necessary.	Manager		
4. Manager gives report to accounting department by 25th of the month.	Manager		
5. Amend report to comply with corporate reimbursement guidelines.	Accountant		
6. Check issued by the last day of the month.	Accountant		

MONTH END ACCOUNTING PROCEDURES

Step	Person Responsible	Activity Code	Form Letter
1. Close day for last day of the month.	Accountant		
2. Initiate month end.	Accountant		
3. Run automation system generated JE Report.	Accountant		
4. Run agent reports.	Accountant		
5. Balance Aged Accounts Receivables to GL and distribute to management and agents (also done on 15th of the month).	Accountant		
6. Run Bank Statements & give to reconciler.	President		
7. Enter Fixed Assets into FAS system. Allocate depreciation.	Accountant		
8. Run unapplied Cash Report & distribute to management and CSRs (also done on 15th of the month).	Accountant		
9. Run Aged Accounts Receivables Credit Balances only – Move to payables account.	Accountant		
10. Allocate Payroll to departments and do accruals.	Accountant		
11. Allocate Employee benefit expenses.	Accountant		
12. Amortize acquired agencies.	Accountant		
13. Run Commercial Lines expiration list for four months in advance & give to CSRs.	Accountant		
14. Run Commercial Lines EXPIRED list for month just ended and give to CSRs.	Accountant		
15. Run Personal Lines Expiration list two months in advance & give to appropriate individual.	Accountant		

BANK RECONCILIATIONS

Step	Person Responsible	Activity Code	Form Letter
1. Run Bank Statement on Automation System.	Accountant		
2. Reconcile on automation system if available or do manually.	Anyone other than Accountant		
3. Record Fees & Interest into automation system.	Accountant		
4. Uncashed checks over 60 days old are sent form letter.	Accountant		
5. If no response, send second request with 14-day follow-up. If response, reissue check if necessary.	Accountant		

DIRECT BILL RECONCILIATION

Step	Person Responsible	Activity Code	Form Letter
1. Statement comes in.	File Clerk		
2. Look up the client in automation system	Accountant		
3. Finds the right policy number	Accountant		
4. Invoices the premium & commission percentage	Accountant		
5. Verify commission dollar amount	Accountant		
6. If new business make sure agent & commission percentage is correct.	Accountant		
7. Highlight statement as recorded.	Accountant		
8. Verify that check received equals total of statement recorded.	Accountant		
9. If step #8 does not equal, investigate and correct discrepancies.	Accountant		

LIFE & HEALTH PROCEDURES

INDIVIDUAL LIFE SALES

Step	Person Responsible	Activity Code	Form Letter
1. Call prospect and gather information (needs analysis).	L&H Agent		
2. Get quote from carrier.	L&H CSR		
3. Put together proposal within 5 days of receiving quote.	L&H CSR		
4. Meet with prospect to present proposal.	L&H Agent		
5. If no, pend as prospect for one month follow-up.	L&H Agent		
6. If yes, go to **Individual Life New Business** Process.			

INDIVIDUAL HEALTH NEW BUSINESS

Step	Person Responsible	Activity Code	Form Letter
1. Quote the premium	L&H Agent		
2. Complete application.	L&H Agent		
3. Review application for completeness.	L&H CSR		
4. Enter into automation system as client.	L&H CSR		
5. Send application to Carrier and make copy.	L&H CSR		
6. Pend until policy is issued.	L&H CSR		
7. Policy comes in.	L&H CSR		
8. Update application in automation system.	L&H CSR		
9. File copy of application and policy.	L&H CSR		

Page 13 of 28

INDIVIDUAL LIFE NEW BUSINESS

Step	Person Responsible	Activity Code	Form Letter
1. Complete the application	L&H Agent		
2. Turn in completed application to CSR.	L&H Agent		
3. Review application and add agent code to the application.	L&H CSR		
4. Set up as CLIENT in automation system.	L&H CSR		
5. Make sure any additional forms are completed and attached.	L&H CSR		
6. Order exam	L&H CSR		
7. Fax and or mail application with memo. Copy of application is filed in pending.	L&H CSR		
8. Check carrier system for activity & note in automation system.	L&H CSR		
9. Every Wednesday the agent is to be emailed as to status.	L&H CSR		
10. Respond to additional info requests.	L&H CSR		
11. If re-rated: repropose to client.	L&H Agent		
12. Present to client. If NO, stop & set up to move client to prospect status.	L&H Agent		
13. If YES, order policy to be issued.	L&H CSR		
14. Policy comes in. Compare application, if errors, request reissue. If good, copy important pages. Tell agent if there are requirements to be signed.	L&H CSR		
15. Update Dec page & info screens in automation system.	L&H CSR		
16. Requirements come in	L&H Agent		
17. Send policy and requirements page(s) to agent.	L&H CSR		
18. Return requirements pages to CSR.	L&H Agent		
19. Copy signed requirements page and file it.	L&H CSR		
20. Send memo and requirements page to Carrier.	L&H CSR		

Managing Human Resources in an Insurance Agency **177**

COMMERCIAL LINES PROCEDURES

COMMERCIAL LINES NEW BUSINESS QUOTATION - LARGE ACCOUNTS

Step	Person Responsible	Activity Code	Form Letter
All applications must be signed by client, no exceptions!			
1. Completed application (enough for underwriter to quote) sent to the Marketing Manager at least 60 days in advance of expiration. Include instructions on preferred carriers	CL Agent		
2. Add as a prospect in the automation system. Input application into computer to quote it in house or submit to carriers. Apprise agent every 10 days as to status.	Marketing Manager		
3. Call agent if additional information is needed. I.e. loss run, driver list, photos, etc.	Marketing Manager		
4. Gather additional info and return.	CL Agent		
5. When the quote comes in, verify quote information against your request.	Marketing Manager		
6. Advise agent as quotes come in.	Marketing Manager		
7. Prepare proposal.	CL CSR		
8. Go to CL PROPOSAL PRESENTATION			

COMMERCIAL LINES NEW BUSINESS QUOTATION - SMALL ACCOUNTS

Step	Person Responsible	Activity Code	Form Letter
All applications must be signed by client, no exceptions!			
1. Gather information from client.	CL Producer		
2. Add as a prospect in the automation system. Input application into computer.	CL CSR		
3. Gather additional information if needed, i.e., loss run, driver list, photos, etc.	CL Producer		
4. Generate new quote.	CL CSR		
5. Go to CL PROPOSAL PRESENTATION			

COMMERCIAL LINES PROPOSAL PRESENTATION

Step	Person Responsible	Activity Code	Form Letter
1. Prepare presentation	CL CSR and Producer		
2. Present proposal to client	CL Producer		
3. If policy not sold, close open activities, file application, and pend for next year.	CL CSR		
4. Policy is sold. Insured signs proposal to acknowledge coverage. Pick up money. Without a written exception by management, no coverage can be bound without collecting a downpayment. Attempt to finance all agency-billed accounts.	CL Producer		
5. Change from prospect to client in automation system.	CL CSR		
6. Issue certificates, binders, and/or auto ID cards.	CL CSR		
7. Invoice for money already collected on agency-billed policies.	CL CSR		
8. Give certificates, binders, & ID cards to agent to deliver or use cover letter if mailed.	CL CSR		
9. Issue instructions to carrier with changes or issue as is. If necessary, update application on automation system.	CL CSR		
10. File application and quotes together.	CL CSR		
11. Policy comes in.	CL CSR		
12. Review policy against automation system, billing screen, detail screen, application screen, etc.	Processor		
13. If carrier error, fax or email change request to carrier and input open suspense item for receipt of correction. If agency error, correct in automation system.	CL CSR		
14. If correct, generate new business letter.	Processor		
15. Advise producer that policy is in. Determine delivery method (mail or hand delivery). All policies must be delivered within 10 days of receipt.	CL CSR		
16. File agency's copy of policy.	Processor		

Page 16 of 28

COMMERCIAL LINES AGENCY RENEWALS

Step	Person Responsible	Activity Code	Form Letter
1. As part of end-of-month accounting runs an expiration list by CSR for four months in advance and distributes to CSRs.	Accountant		
2. CSRs work on large and/or complex accounts first.	CL CSR		
3. CSR produced an updated future application.	CL CSR		
4. Print future application and give to producer.	CL CSR		
5. Gather updated information, or ask CSR to gather information on smaller accounts.	CL Producer		
6. Print certificate holder lists, schedule of vehicles, list of equipment, etc., and forward to insured for review and update.	CL CSR		
7. If remarketing, order loss runs	CL CSR		
8. CSR gets application back from agent with changes (or contacts client if CSR is gathering information).	CL CSR		
9. If large account, when the quote comes in, verify quote information against application. Otherwise generate quote internally.	CL CSR		
10. Go to CL PROPOSAL PRESENTATION			

COMMERCIAL LINES CARRIER RENEWALS (Direct Bill)

Step	Person Responsible	Activity Code	Form Letter
1. If agency has not received renewal one month prior to expiration, call carrier..	CL CSR		
2. Once received, check renewal off expiration list.	CL CSR		
3. Update all sections of the application and request any necessary changes from carrier.	CL CSR		
4. Update certificate(s).	Processor		
5. Send original(s) to certificate holder(s).	Processor		
6. Send copy certificate(s) to client along with Auto ID cards if needed.	Processor		
7. Compare policy to automation system detail.	Processor		
8. Update billing screen (change amounts, etc.)	Processor		
9. Edit and print commercial lines renewal letter. .	Processor		
10. File agency's copy.	Processor		
11. Close out all related activities out.	CL CSR		

COMMERCIAL LINES CARRIER RENEWALS (Agency Billed)

Step	Person Responsible	Activity Code	Form Letter
1. Call carrier if renewal has not been received by agency one month prior to expiration.	CL CSR		
2. Once policy is received, check off expiration list.	CL CSR		
3. Update future application and request any necessary changes.	CL CSR Assistant		
4. Issue invoice(30 days in advance of renewal date).	CL CSR		
5. Two weeks prior to expiration send a 2nd request if payment is not received.	CL CSR		
6. When policy comes in, compare it to automation system detail (billing screen, activity screen, future application screen). Make sure all changes appear on future application screen.	Processor		
7. Notify producer that policy has come in and is being held until payment is received	CL CSR		
8. If payment is not received by expiration, return policy for flat cancellation.	CL CSR		
9. If payment received, update certificate(s).	CL CSR		
10. Send original(s) to certificate holder(s).	CL CSR		
11. Deliver policy (by mail or personally by Producer) to client along with Auto ID cards if needed and copies of certificates.	CL Producer or CSR		
12. If mailing, print cover letter and send any ID cards and copies of certificates.	Processor		
13. File agent's copy of policy.	Processor		
14. Close out all related activities.	CL CSR		

Page 18 of 28

RENEWING SURPLUS LINES ACCOUNTS

Step	Person Responsible	Activity Code	Form Letter
1. Review expiration list 90 days in advance of renewal. Check availability of coverage through standard markets.	CL CSR		
2. Contact surplus lines carriers for renewal application if required.	CL CSR		
3. Complete generic information and give to producer.	CL CSR		
4. Review and update information with insured.	CL Agent		
5. Fax application with cover letter to surplus lines carrier. Fax to multiple carriers if producer wants account marketed.	CL CSR		
6. Pend application until renewal is received.	CL CSR		
7. If quote not received in 10 days, call carrier(s) to check status. REPEND for one week.	CL CSR		
8. Quote comes in. Review with agent.	CL CSR		
9. Set up finance contract if needed.	CL CSR		
10. Prepare renewal proposal.	CL CSR		
11. Give finance agreement & renewal proposal to producer to present to client.	CL CSR		
12. Deliver renewal proposal and finance agreement to client.	CL Producer		
13. Receive signed application, signed finance agreement, and deposit premium.	CL CSR		
14. Send application to carrier with request to bind coverage and send binder to client.	CL CSR		
15. File outstanding correspondence.	CL CSR		
16. Send finance agreement to finance carrier and give deposit check to accounting.	CL CSR		
17. Close out prior related activities.	CL CSR		
18. Policy comes in. Mail to client (or delivered by Agent) with cover letter stating that policy is not covered by state guarantee fund.	CL CSR		
19. File all related correspondence.	CL CSR		

COMMERCIAL LINES ENDORSEMENTS & CHANGES

Step	Person Responsible	Activity Code	Form Letter
1. CSR takes call from client or agent.	CL CSR		
2. If using service center, transfer call to carrier service center, or gather information and call it into carrier service center. Changes are downloaded into automation system.	CL CSR		
3. If no service center, CSR does change request screen. Make sure future application has been updated. Save to history on effective date. Print change request form, forward to carrier for processing, and pend for receipt of endorsement.	CL CSR		
4. Send second request if necessary & repend.	CL CSR		
5. When endorsement comes in close activity.	CL CSR		
6. Verify endorsement against change request.	CL CSR		
7. (On agency bill) If change request is incorrect, contact carrier to correct. Hold original until correction is received.	CL CSR		
8. Do form letter. Specify what endorsement does and amount of premium if direct bill. If agency bill, invoice premium and set activity for follow-up of payment.	CL CSR		
9. Mail endorsement to client.	CL CSR		
10. File and close all related activities.	CLCSR		

COMMERCIAL LINES CLAIMS

Step	Person Responsible	Activity Code	Form Letter
1. Call comes in, transfer call to Claims Manager.	CL CSR		
2. Open claim screen and gather information.	Claims Manager		
3. Print loss notice form. Fax or call loss notice to carrier.	Claims Manager		
4. If suit papers come in, forward to carrier.	Claims Manager		
5. Receive acknowledgement from carrier regarding loss notice and/or suit papers.	Claims Manager		
6. If acknowledgement is not received within three days, contact carrier to assure loss notice / suit papers were received.	Claims Manager		
7. Update claim detail screen.	Claims Manager		
8. File acknowledgement.	Claims Manager		
9. Follow up on claim status every two weeks until conclusion.	Claims Manager		
10. When payment acknowledgement comes in, input into claims payment screen.	Claims Manager		
11. File payment notice.	Claims Manager		

Page 21 of 28

COMMERCIAL LINES AUDITS

Step	Person Responsible	Activity Code	Form Letter
Return all uncollected audits within 30 days even if carrier allows more than 30 days.			
1. Audit is received from carrier.	CL CSR		
2. Check audit for accuracy. If incorrect, return to carrier with explanation of error. Pend 30 days for receipt of revised audit. Follow up as needed.	CL CSR		
3. Enter the audit information into the agency management system. Invoice if agency bill.	CL CSR		
4. If over $500 discuss with producer.	CL CSR		
5. If under $500 mail audit and invoice to client with form letter. Pend for 15 days	CL CSR		
6. File original	CL CSR		
7. If payment is not made, call client to see if audit is disputed or if it is going to be paid. If disputed, Email producer to resolve, otherwise collect or return to company.	CL CSR		
8. If Agent does not respond or fails to collect in 3 days return audit to carrier.	CL CSR		

COMMERCIAL LINES DIRECT BILL CANCELLATIONS & REINSTATEMENTS (For Non-Payment)

Step	Person Responsible	Activity Code	Form Letter
1. Separate all cancellation notices from mail.	Mail Clerk		
2. Enter notice information into agency management system. Enter description with reason, amount, effective date, etc.	Processor		
3. Call Direct Bill 800 line to see if money has been received. If yes, close out activity.	Processor		
4. If no, do nothing (inconsistently calling client can result in E&O exposure).	Processor		
5. Upon receipt of reinstatement, record information as an activity in the agency management system. Close the open activity related to the cancellation notice.	Processor		
6. If final cancellation notice is received, notify producer.	Processor		
7. Prepare cancellation notice letter and mail to insured. Change policy status in agency management system to cancelled.	Processor		
8. Close the open activity related to the cancellation notice.	Processor		
9. If this was the only policy in force for this client, change customer status to inactive.	Processor		

Page 22 of 28

COMMERCIAL LINES CANCELLATIONS
(Insured's Request)

Step	Person Responsible	Activity Code	Form Letter
1. Insured contacts agency and requests cancellation. Ask insured reason for cancellation and enter information into agency management system.	CL CSR		
2. Mail or fax Lost Policy Release (LPR) form along with form letter. Enter an activity to follow up in 10 days.	CL CSR		
3. Email notice to Producer.	CL CSR		
4. Second request LPR if necessary.	CL CSR		
5. LPR form comes in. Record receipt as an activity with an open follow-up.	CL CSR		
6. Mail original LPR to carrier	CL CSR		
7. File copy of LPR.	CL CSR		
8. Cancellation verification comes in from carrier.	CL CSR		
9. Process cancellation, invoice if agency billed and additional premium due to audit. If return premium order refund check from accounting department.	CL CSR		

PERSONAL LINES PROCEDURES

QUOTING NEW PERSONAL LINES PROSPECTS

Step	Person Responsible	Activity Code	Form Letter
1. Call comes in. Determine and record source of call and refer to appropriates producer for evaluation and quote.	Receptionist		
2. Check automation system prospect and client screens, if new set up new prospect. If existing & activity within 180 days give to original producer. If existing & activity beyond 180 days, agent catching call gets to keep.	PL Producer		
3. Determine eligibility according to agency guidelines.	PL Producer		
4. Add prospect into the agency automation system.	PL Producer		
5. Develop policy quotation through agency or company software. Order CLU and MVR as necessary.	PL Producer		
6. Prepare quote. Upload the quoted policy to the prospect file in the agency management system.	PL Producer		
7. Present quote to prospect. If declined, stop.	PL Producer		
8. If accepted, go to PERSONAL LINES APPLICATION PROCEDURE.			

PERSONAL LINES APPLICATION PROCEDURE

Step	Person Responsible	Activity Code	Form Letter
1. When quote is accepted by client, explain the application and binding procedure. Schedule appointment for the completion of the application.	PL Producer		
2. Convert status from Prospect to Client in agency management system.	PL Producer		
3. Create application. Obtain applicant's signature on application and all necessary supplemental forms.	PL Producer		
4. Collect deposit premium.	PL Producer		
5. Create documentation for applicant as required (i.e. auto ID cards, binder, certificate of insurance, etc.) Forward copies to appropriate parties (such as mortgagee).	PL Processor		
6. Forward application and deposit premium (via check or bank sweep) to the carrier the same day, or upload into company system.	PL Processor		
7. Create an open activity to follow up for receipt of policy.	PL Processor		
8. File application and quote information.	PL Processor		
9. Send new business thank you letter to client.	PL Processor		
10. Follow up with carrier if policy is not received by follow up date (#7 above), pend for appropriate follow up.	PL Processor		
11. Go to PERSONAL LINES NEW POLICY RECEIPT PROCEDURE.			

PERSONAL LINES NEW POLICY RECEIPT PROCEDURE

Step	Person Responsible	Activity Code	Form Letter
1. New policy is received. Verify for accuracy against application and system information.	PL CSR		
2. Enter policy information and/or corrections into agency management system and request any necessary corrections.	PL CSR		
3. Invoice premium if necessary.	PL CSR		
4. If agency received insured's copy of policy, forward to insured within seven days of receipt by agency.	PL CSR		
5. File agency copy of policy.	PL CSR		
6. Close any open activities.	PL CSR		

PERSONAL LINES NON-RENEWALS

Step	Person Responsible	Activity Code	Form Letter
Non-Renewals by Carrier			
1. Carrier notifies client and agency of non-renewal.	Carrier		
2. Send letter to client to contact agency.	PL CSR		
3. If client would like agency to remarket coverage, update underwriting information with insured and follow renewal instructions (See Commercial Lines Carrier Renewal (Direct Bill) procedures).	PL Agent		

PERSONAL LINES CLAIMS

(See COMMERCIAL LINES CLAIMS procedure)

PERSONAL LINES ENDORSEMENTS & CHANGES

Step	Person Responsible	Activity Code	Form Letter
1. Client calls to request change. If policy is handled by a carrier service center, forward call to the service center. If not, proceed with the following steps.	PL CSR		
2. Go into application under change request and add a new change request. Effective date is today unless client requests differently.	PL CSR		
3. Document under remarks and reference why change was made. If change request is initiated by any party other than the named insured, confirm with the insured before making any significant change in coverage. If insured requests coverage to be reduced, obtain signature on rejection form.	PL CSR		
4. Print endorsement request.	PL CSR		
5. Call / fax / mail carriers to process the change and pend for receipt of endorsement. If agency uploads policy changes with a carrier, process the change in the company system.	PL CSR		
6. Only file paperwork if client has signed a form to reduce coverage, otherwise discard.	PL CSR		
7. Call carrier if not received in 30 days, repend if necessary.	PL CSR		
8. Review downloaded endorsement or paper documentation.	PL CSR		
9. If endorsement is correct, close activity and file paperwork.	PL CSR		
10. If endorsement is incorrect, close original activity.	PL CSR		
11. Open new activity to correct endorsement, forward correction to carrier.	PL CSR		
12. Go to step #7.	PL CSR		

PERSONAL LINES CANCELLATIONS

Step	Person Responsible	Activity Code	Form Letter
At insureds request:			
1. Complete cancellation form including date of cancellation and reason for cancellation.	PL CSR		
2. Send form to client for signature.	PL CSR		
3. If not received in 7 days, send second request.	PL CSR		
4. Form comes in. Close activity and send form (via mail or fax) to carrier. File photocopy of form.	PL CSR		
5. Wait for final carrier acknowledgement.	PL CSR		
6. If not received in 30 days, call carrier and resubmit from file. Extend follow-up date.	PL CSR		
7. When carrier acknowledgement is received, record receipt including effective date and file. If applicable, request refund to be issued by accounting department. Zero out premium on detail screen and change status.	PL CSR		
8. Record and move policy to history.	PL CSR		
9. Via download: Follow paper procedures but verify cancellation request to automation system download.	PL CSR		
If cancelled by the carrier due to lack of information:			
1. Receive request for additional information.	Mail Clerk		
2. Give request to CSR.	Mail clerk		
3. If renewal: CSR calls or generates memo to client requesting information. If New Business, forward to producer to gather information. CSR to leave an open activity and follow up every three days until information is received.	PL CSR		
4. When information comes in, forward to carrier. Keep an open activity and pend/follow up until reinstatement is received.	PL CSR		
5. When reinstatement is received, verify accuracy, address any coverage gaps with the company and communicate to insured.	PL CSR		

Website References

Section 1: Hiring & Firing

Candidate Sources

National Insurance Recruiters Association   www.nirassn.com

National Association of Insurance Women   www.naiw.net

Job search websites   www.monster.com
www.hotjobs.com

Background Checks

The Omnia Group   www.omnia720.com/products/backgroundchecks.asp

Training & Development

National Alliance   www.TheNationalAlliance.com

Section 2: Employment Laws

Fair Labor Standards Act

www.dol.gov/elaws/flsa.htm
www.dol.gov/esa/
www.opm.gov/flsa/overview.asp

Equal Pay Act

www.eeoc.gov/policy/epa.html
www.eeoc.gov/epa/

Title VII of the Civil Rights Act

www.eeoc.gov/policy/vii.html

Age Discrimination in Employment Act

www.eeoc.gov/policy/adea.html
www.eeoc.gov/facts/age.html

Federal Wiretapping Act

www.monnat.com/Publications/Wiretap.pdf

Fair Credit Reporting Act

www.ftc.gov/os/statutes/fcra.htm

Credit Reporting Companies

www.transunion.com
www.equifax.com
www.experian.com

Pregnancy Discrimination Act

www.eeoc.gov/facts/fs-preg.html

Consolidated Budget Omnibus
Reconciliation Act (COBRA)

www.dol.gov/dol/topic/health-plans/cobra.htm
www.dol.gov/ebsa/faqs/faq_consumer_cobra.html

Immigration Reform & Control Act

www.usda.gov/agency/oce/oce/labor-affairs/
ircasumm.htm

Employee Polygraph Protection Act

www.fas.org/sgp/othergov/polygraph/eppa.html
www.dol.gov/esa/regs/statutes/whd/poly01.pdf

American with Disabilities Act

www.usdoj.gov/crt/ada/adahom1.htm

Family Medical Leave Act

www.dol.gov/esa/whd/fmla/

Human Resources Related Courses

The following courses are available through the National Alliance for Insurance Education & Research. For more detailed information or to register go to www.TheNationalAlliance.com or call 800-633-2165

Agency Management Institute

This institute covers the important internal operations and factors that are necessary to successfully run an agency in today's business world.

Topics:

- The Agency as an Organization

- Financial Analysis

- Human Resources

- Legal and Ethical Responsibilities

- Managing Your Book of Business

- Agency Productivity and Effectiveness

Participants will:

- Learn to balance the roles of professional insurance counselor and successful businessperson.

- Find methods to build and maintain staff support, maximize customer service, and improve overall operations while increasing the agency's bottom line.

Agency Management Practices Ruble Seminar

This seminar helps you develop the ability, knowledge and time to effectively and continually manage all aspects of the business on a daily basis and still have the leadership ability, motivation, time, and vision to provide direction. You can choose your specific area of interest during one concurrent-topic session.

Topics:

- Comparing your agency's performance to new industry-wide benchmarks

- Isolating variances through in-depth financial analysis

- Auditing your agency's automation efficiency

- Identifying what is being done correctly, and targeting areas for improved automation marketing

- Discovering the legal responsibilities of the agency owner as an employer

- Adapting customer service to an automated environment

- Understanding what's involved in perpetuations, mergers and acquisitions, and agency valuations

Managing People Ruble Seminar

This practical seminar will help build skills to improve your human resource strategies and develop your leadership style to move the agency forward. Learn to read employees' personality styles to bring out their greatest potential.

Topics:

- Proactive ways to understand the behavioral styles of employees

- Methods for creating cohesive work units and improving communication

- Assessing your agency's human resources strategies

- Enhancing productivity and job satisfaction

- The dynamics of leadership

Note: Ruble Seminars are only available to dues-paid CICs and CRMs.

About the Author

Jon Persky, CIC, CPA, PHR

Jon Persky graduated from Duquesne University, holds an MBA in Finance from the University of Pittsburgh, is a Certified Public Accountant, a Certified Insurance Counselor, and holds the Professional in Human Resources designation from the Society of Human Resource Management.

He has spent the majority of his professional career in the insurance industry, in positions such as Controller, Chief Financial Officer, and Personnel Director. The agencies Jon has been associated with range from a large commercial-lines-only agency to a 35-location non-standard auto agency. Jon has also been the Vice President of Operations of a law firm.

Jon is the President of Optimum Performance Solutions, LLC, a company that provides management consulting on a nationwide basis to insurance agencies. The firm specializes in the areas of mergers and acquisitions, agency valuation and perpetuation planning.

In addition to being the author of this publication, he is also the author of *Maximizing Agency Value II: A Guide for Buying, Selling, and Perpetuating Insurance Agencies*, available from the Academy of Producer Insurance Studies. Jon is also the endorsed consultant for several state insurance associations.

About The Academy
Practical Research for Insurance Professionals

Founded in 1983, The National Alliance Research Academy is a research organization that supplies practical research for insurance and risk management professionals. The Academy is a non-profit, publicly-supported corporation governed by a board of insurance professionals. The goals of The Academy are:

- To conduct research of practical value and significant interest to insurance and risk management professionals and their staff.
- To become the leading source of insurance agency performance standards and ratios through regular publication of *Growth and Performance Standards*.
- To provide a forum for insurance and risk management professionals to exchange ideas, participate in research, and have research published.
- To be a continuing source of new curricula and lecture material for the Society of CIC, the Society of CISR, and Certified Risk Managers (CRM) International.

Membership

Membership Categories
- **Fellow:** $15. Designated CICs, CISRs, and CRMs who are dues-paying members of the Society of CIC or CISR, or CRM International.
- **Associate:** $35. An individual who is not currently a dues-paying member of the Society of CIC or CISR, or CRM International.
- **Research Associate:** $1,000. A corporate entity or association.

Enjoy the Benefits of Academy Membership:
- A 10% discount on all Academy publications.
- A regular copy of *Resources* magazine, a great source of valuable technical information, and schedules of all National Alliance programs.
- The research bulletin, *Preliminary Findings*, sent to you periodically with new discoveries and statistics based on Academy works in progress.
- The opportunity to participate in upcoming studies and receive Executive Summaries of the results.

For More Information About The Academy

The National Alliance Research Academy
P.O. Box 27027, Austin, Texas 78755-2027
Phone: 800-633-2165
Fax: 512-349-6194
Email: alliance@scic.com
Online: www.TheNationalAlliance.com

Academy Publications

Please check the website for current publications and prices: www.TheNationalAlliance.com.

Coverage Series

The Three Faces of Executive Liability: D&O, EPL, and Fiduciary Exposures and Coverages (second edition)

Gain a valuable understanding of the exposures, coverages, and risk management techniques regarding Directors and Officers Liability, Employment Practices Liability, and Fiduciary Liability. Benefit from the author's extensive knowledge and experience to analyze risks, prepare proposals, and evaluate coverage needs for clients and prospects. 81 pages

The Insurance Essentials Handbook: Personal Lines, Commercial Property & Casualty

Learn the basic insurance terms, concepts, coverages, and exclusions for P&C insurance. Focus on the key aspects of Homeowners, Commercial General Liability, Workers Compensation, and other pertinent topics. Practical examples are provided throughout to aid in explanation and increase understanding for less experienced insurance professionals. 382 pages

Productivity Series

The Producer Profile: Compensation, Production, and Responsibilities

Compare producers' compensation, production, responsibilities, and experience — for both commercial and personal lines producers. Use checklists, job descriptions, producer agreements, and detailed information — such as average salary, typical benefits, and annual sales production — to compare yourself or other producers in your agency to national survey results. 211 pages

The CSR Profile: Facing Challenges in Customer Service

Draw upon the experience of other CSRs to compare your compensation, servicing volume, and responsibilities. Read about qualifications, experience, skills, and knowledge for both commercial and personal lines CSRs. Based on a nationwide survey, this study is geared towards CSRs, agency owners, and personnel managers.

Growth and Performance Standards (GPS) 2002-2003

Compare to income and expense averages, productivity measures, and balance sheet ratios of other agencies based on size and region. Discover how well the best performing agencies are doing, and gauge the results of agencies that focus on either commercial or personal lines business. Use the companion CD to compare your numbers, compute variances, and improve results. 146 pages

Fee-Based Services: Using Fees to Increase Revenues and Retain Accounts

Explore the benefits and obstacles in providing fee-based services, and discover revenue opportunities with different types of services, risk management issues, and accounts. Refer to this in-depth study for guidance in determining costs and pricing considerations, along with implementation issues. 78 pages

Transactional Filing: An Integrated Approach

Determine the benefits, and disadvantages, of transactional filing by date, rather than by client name. Take advantage of the author's knowledge and experience to help you in the transition to this type of filing system. 40 pages

Understanding the Wholesale Insurance Market

This study will help retail agencies develop continuing, effective relationships with wholesale brokers and agencies. Likewise, wholesalers can improve their procedures and upgrade their opportunities with retail agencies. Receive additional advice about selection and authority of both wholesale and retail agencies. 82 pages

Imaging at a Glance

This study helps agencies to implement an efficient process for the scanning and electronic storage of documents. This monograph, complete with agency survey results, allows agencies to improve productivity, minimize difficulties, implement an appropriate system, and assign staff responsibilities. 72 pages

The 25 Most Innovative Agents in America

Review the profiles of 25 outstanding insurance agents who tell their stories in a collection of visionary examples. Their success secrets may inspire you to be more creative in your own career. 155 pages

Marketing Series

Maximizing Agency Value II: A Guide for Buying, Selling, and Perpetuating Insurance Agencies

Investigate the key issues and decisions involved in buying and selling an agency. Use detailed sample agreements, letters, and checklists to assist with these processes. Follow steps to analyze other agencies, as well as your own, to maximize current value and future net worth. 235 pages

Zoom In On Sales: Target Marketing, Prospecting, and Sales Centers

Improve your target marketing and prospecting results. Organize your marketing and sales activities by operating a sales center. Agency survey results and resources on CD — sample letters, telemarketing scripts, activity tracking forms, and sample job descriptions make this a practical guide. 118 pages

Dynamics of Selling Audio Series

Refresh, renew, and reinforce your selling skills. Learn how to super qualify prospects, build rapport, probe for needs, overcome objections, and master the selling sequence. Energize your sales process with this learning and reinforcement tool.

Terms and Conditions of Use

PLEASE READ THESE TERMS AND CONDITIONS CAREFULLY BEFORE USING THE CD-ROM AND THE CONTENTS THEREOF.

The "Managing Human Resources in an Insurance Agency" publication, and this and other accompanying CD-ROMs and contents (collectively, the "Content"), is made available by The Academy for Producer Insurance Studies, Inc. D.B.A. The National Alliance Research Academy, a Texas corporation ("Academy"), and may be used only under the following terms and conditions.

BY ACCESSING AND USING the CONTENT (including without limitation the "Managing Human Resources in an Insurance Agency" publication, its information, this CD-ROM and any other accompanying CD-ROM, INformation, and forms), you ("User") AGREE TO BE LEGALLY BOUND BY THE TERMS AND CONDITIONS SET FORTH HEREIN (the "Agreement").

1. **License.** User is granted a non-exclusive, non-transferable, revocable, limited license to access and use the Content (including, the information, forms, and other matter of the Content) for personal, non-commercial purposes and use.

2. **Limitations.** User may not copy, download, store, publish, transmit, transfer, sell, sublicense or other use the Content, or any portion thereof, in any form or by any means, except (i) as expressly permitted by this Agreement, (ii) with Academy's prior written permission, or (iii) if not expressly prohibited by this Agreement, as allowed under the fair use provision of the Copyright Act (17 U.S.C. §107). User may not alter or modify information provided in the Content in any way; provided, User may copy a single copy of the Content to an electronic storage of a single computer for personal, non-commercial use and may modify the Content on the electronic storage of the single computer only if modified for personal, non-commercial use and for the User's sole access. User may not reverse engineer, decompile, disassemble or otherwise attempt to discern the source code or architecture of the software and operational Content of the CD-ROMs.

3. **Intellectual Property Rights.** User acknowledges and agrees that the Content and each publication made available by Academy are owned exclusively by Academy and are protected by copyrights, trademarks, service marks, patents and other proprietary rights and laws. Nothing herein shall be construed to confer any license or right, by implication, estoppel, or otherwise, under copyright or other intellectual property rights.

4. **No Legal Advice and No Practice of Law.** Academy provides the Content for informational purposes only. User acknowledges that under no circumstances is Academy, its agents, affiliates, or customers, providing legal advice or representation by so providing the Content, and that nothing within the Content and nothing with regard to the provision of the Content by Academy is intended as or should be used or considered as a substitute for legal advice from an attorney or as a substitute for tax, business or other advice from a tax or other professional. Academy disclaims all responsibility for User's access and use of the Content.

5. **User Representations and Warranties.** User agrees, upon request by Academy, to provide Academy with accurate, complete information regarding all aspects and circumstances of User's access and use of the Content. User represents and warrants that User's access and use is for a single person only, and that User will not permit anyone other than User to access and use the Content. User will notify Academy immediately of any unauthorized use of the Content. User represents and warrants that the Content will be used to provide general information only, and not for provision of legal advice or the practice of law.

6. **Third Party Content.** Third party content, including that of authors and editors, may be incorporated in the Content or may be accessible from or with use of the Content. Academy is not responsible, and assumes no liability, for third party content, including, without limitation, for any third party mistakes, misstatements of law, defamation, slander, libel, omissions, falsehood, misrepresentation, or misunderstanding in the statements, thoughts, opinions, representations or any other information within, accessible from, expressed or implied by, or otherwise contained or included in the Content.

7. DISCLAIMER OF WARRANTY. THE CONTENT, INCLUDING THE PUBLICATION, THE CD-ROM(S) AND THE INFORMATION THEREIN AND THEREFROM, IS PROVIDED "AS IS", WITHOUT WARRANTY OF ANY KIND, EXPRESS OR IMPLIED. TO THE FULLEST EXTENT PERMISSIBLE UNDER APPLICABLE LAW, ACADEMY, ITS AGENTS, AFFILIATES, CUSTOMERS, CONTRIBUTORS AND REPRESENTATIVES, DISCLAIMS ALL WARRANTIES, EXPRESS OR IMPLIED, INCLUDING BUT NOT LIMITED TO, WARRANTIES OF PERFORMANCE, MERCHANTABILITY, FITNESS FOR A PARTICULAR PURPOSE, ACCURACY, OMMISSIONS, COMPLETENESS, CURRENTNESS, DELAYS AND OTHERWISE. ACADEMY MAKES NO WARRANTY THAT ACCESS TO OR USE OF THE CONTENT, OR ANY PORTION THEREOF, WILL BE COMPLETE, ERROR FREE, CORRECT, OR THAT DEFECTS WILL BE CORRECTED. ACADEMY DISCLAIMS ALL RESPONSIBILITY, WHATSOEVER, FOR ANY LOSS, INJURY, CLAIM, LIABILITY, OR DAMAGE OF ANY KIND RESULTING FROM, ARISING OUT OF, OR IN ANY WAY RELATED TO THE PROVISION, ACCESS OR USE OF THE CONTENT OR USER'S USE OF EQUIPMENT AND SOFTWARE IN CONNECTION WITH SUCH PROVISION, ACCESS AND USE.

8. LIMITATION OF LIABILITY. USER'S EXCLUSIVE REMEDY AND ACADEMY'S, ITS AGENTS, AFFILITATES, CUSTOMERS, CONTRIBUTORS AND REPRESENTATIVES, ENTIRE LIABILITY UNDER THIS AGREEMENT AND IN CONNECTION WITH PROVISION AND USER'S USE AND ACCESS OF THE CONTENT (IF ANY SUCH LIABILITY) FOR ANY CLAIM FOR DAMAGES RELATING TO THE PROVISION, USE AND ACCESS OF THE CONTENT, SHALL BE LIMITED TO THE AGGREGATE AMOUNT OF CHARGES PAID BY USER (IF ANY SO PAID) FOR THE SPECIFIC CONTENT FEATURE WHICH IS THE BASIS OF THE CLAIM DURING THE 12 MONTH PERIOD PRECEDING THE EVENT GIVING RISE TO SUCH CLAIM. IN NO EVENT SHALL ACADEMY, ITS AGENTS, AFFILIATES, CUSTOMERS, CONTRIBUTORS OR REPRESENTATIVES, BE LIABLE TO USER FOR ANY CLAIM RELATING IN ANY WAY TO (A) USER'S ACCESS OR USE OF THE CONTENT, OR ANY DECISION MADE OR ACTION TAKEN BY USER IN RELIANCE ON THE CONTENT; OR (B) ANY LOST PROFITS OR CONSEQUENTIAL, EXEMPLARY, INCIDENTAL, INDIRECT OR SPECIAL DAMAGES RELATING IN WHOLE OR PART TO USER'S RIGHTS AND OBLIGATIONS UNDER THIS AGREEMENT OR PROVISION, ACCESS, USE OF, OR INABILITY TO ACCESS OR USE, THE CONTENT, EVEN IF Academy, OR ANY OF ITS AGENTS, AFFILITATES, CUSTOMERS, CONTRIBUTORS OR REPRESENTATIVES, HAS BEEN ADVISED OF THE POSSIBLITY OF SUCH DAMAGES. ACADEMY SHALL HAVE NO LIABILITY WHATSOEVER TO USER FOR ANY CLAIM RELATING IN ANY WAY TO ANY THIRD PARTY CONTENT OR FEATURE.

9. **Modifications to Terms of Use.** Academy reserves the right to terminate or modify this Agreement at any time. Continued access or use by User of the Content after any such modification to this Agreement constitutes User's assent to such modification.

10. **General Provisions.** This Agreement shall be governed by and construed under the law of the State of Texas, USA, without regard to conflicts of law provisions. The parties agree that the state and federal courts in Austin, Travis County, Texas, shall have sole and exclusive jurisdiction over any claim arising out of this Agreement, and each party consents to the sole and exclusive jurisdiction of such courts. Neither this Agreement, nor any part or portion of this Agreement or the Content, may be assigned, sublicensed, or otherwise transferred by User without Academy's prior written consent. If any provision of this Agreement is held to be void, invalid, unenforceable or illegal by a court, the validity and enforceability of the other provisions will not be affected thereby. Failure or delay of any party to enforce any provision of this Agreement will not constitute or be construed as a waiver of such provision or of the right to enforce such provision.